Leighton Parks

His Star in the East

Leighton Parks

His Star in the East

ISBN/EAN: 9783337038496

Printed in Europe, USA, Canada, Australia, Japan

Cover: Foto ©Lupo / pixelio.de

More available books at **www.hansebooks.com**

His Star in the East

A STUDY IN THE EARLY ARYAN RELIGIONS

BY

LEIGHTON PARKS

RECTOR OF EMMANUEL CHURCH, BOSTON

Children of men! the unseen Power, whose eye
Forever doth accompany mankind,
Hath looked on no religion scornfully
That man did ever find.

Which has not taught weak wills how much they can,
Which has not fallen on the dry heart like rain,
Which has not cried to sunk, self weary man:
Thou must be born again!
MATTHEW ARNOLD.

BOSTON AND NEW YORK
HOUGHTON, MIFFLIN AND COMPANY
The Riverside Press, Cambridge
1887

To

THE MEMORY OF MY FATHER,

MARTIN PHILLIPS PARKS, D. D.

This Book

IS REVERENTLY DEDICATED.

PREFACE.

THE substance of this book was first embodied in a course of Lectures, delivered before the Lowell Institute in the winter of 1885, on "Christianity and the early Aryan Religions." Since then the work has been carefully revised and considerable matter added, — much of it of a nature not fitted for such an occasion, — specially that part in the last chapter which relates to the future of the Church, inasmuch as any criticism of Christians of any particular name would have been improper in a series of lectures in an institution avowedly unsectarian. I have also modified in some respects opinions expressed at that time in regard to the influence of Persian thought upon Hebrew theology, my studies since having led me to feel that certain statements, though probably true, could not be easily verified.

The invitation to deliver these lectures induced me to attempt to put in some systematic order thoughts which had long been exercising my mind and employing my leisure moments. This must be my apology for entering upon such a study without the knowledge of Oriental languages which would enable one to make original research. The task which I set before me was not so ambitious as the title of the Lectures might seem to imply. The translations of the Sacred Books of the East, edited by Professor F. Max Müller, can be found in all large libraries, and make it possible for any one who has the time and taste for such studies to become familiar with the thoughts and hopes and fears of the men of old. If I can lay claim to any advantage in such studies, it must be in an interest awakened some ten or twelve years ago when, traveling in the East with my friend Mr. R. B. Bowler, of Cincinnati, I had an opportunity to see the outward life of the people of China, Japan, and India, and to talk with men who still held to the faith of their fathers. I met with too many men in Japan "given to hospitality," I heard too many stories of the unswerving rectitude of Chinese compradors, I found too many examples of the profound and serious thought of men in India, not to return impressed with the great truth that "in every nation, he that feareth God is accepted of Him." And the result of this experience was that in reading the Vedas and the Upanishads and the Sutras and the Zend-Avesta, I have never thought of them as dead books, but as that which has been the staff of life to "living, breathing, thinking men."

It may be that these experiences have fitted me in some sort to write a book which, without any pretense to learning, will nevertheless help some who have been perplexed by the many problems which arise from the consideration of God's dealing with his children. Among such there are none whom I would be so glad to help as the young student of theology, who perhaps has found that such questions are not congenial to the lecture-room of the seminary. There may be some who, without venturing to apply to themselves St. Paul's words, yet have experienced his disappointment, "They who were of repute imparted nothing to me, but contrariwise!" It may be that they shall find here at least the sympathy for which they long.

The questions considered here have a direct bearing on the problem of missions to the heathen,— questions which are coming to the front with startling rapidity. Before these can be answered, it is necessary that we should be clear in our own minds as to what is meant by "the heathen." An examination of this will lead us to see that they differ as we do, and that there is no ready-made method by which they can be converted to Christ, and that no plan can succeed which does not begin in the faith that God has already been making his voice heard, and that they only can understand the words of Christ who have listened to that voice.[1] The problem of missions, then, will be found to run up, like every great spiritual problem, into the one question: "What think ye of the Christ?" All went well as long as the moral sense of mankind did not revolt from the dogma that every soul that had not heard the gospel should be damned. But no man can be found who believes that to-day. By what rule then, shall they be judged? By what used to be called the light of natural reason, while we who have heard shall be judged by the revelation of the Bible? This might do if we were asking questions about a king who has no personal interest in his subjects, but not when the question is concerning the dealing of a Father with his children. Then we must begin with the faith that He has been speaking to his children all along, and that their sin, like ours, consists in not obeying that gracious voice. Call it the natural reason if you will, but do not say that it differs in kind from revelation, or you will have asserted that of the Father which will be the strongest proof that He is no Father; for a Father wants the salvation of every child, and *must* be giving all the time to each

[1] St. John viii. 43.

child all the knowledge and all the grace that the child is capable of receiving.

It is the record of that revelation to which this book desires to call attention. It is a dreadful thing for any minister of Him who said, "They shall come from the East and from the West and sit down in the kingdom of God," to slander those who are coming, for in so doing they "speak a word against the Holy Ghost" who has been leading them.

There is another class to whom I venture to hope that this book may appeal, and that is those who are asking with deep searchings of heart, "Art thou he that should come, or do we look for another?" That they have been led to ask this question as the result of the sudden awakening to the fact that the Bible is not the limit of revelation, I am sure; it may be that a study of some of the great religions will show them that this is truer than they have dared to admit, and yet at the same time make them feel that it is none the less true that "salvation is of the Jews."

I have not been free from an author's perplexity as to references to books to which he is indebted. I had thought of printing a list of all the works consulted in the preparation of this book, but to the scholar it would seem very short, and to the unlearned it would have no meaning. I have therefore contented myself with indicating the books from which quotations are made. The facts stated here can be easily verified, and the opinions must stand or fall by the judgment of the reader. To such a storehouse of learning as Dr. James Freeman Clarke's "Ten Great Religions" I have of course paid frequent visits; but the two books to which I am specially indebted — not so much perhaps in their relation to this work, as in their general influence upon my mind, predisposing me to look at things as I do — are, Cousin's "Lectures on Modern Philosophy," and "The Religions of the World," by that master in theology, Maurice.

EMMANUEL CHURCH, BOSTON.
Epiphany, 1887.

CONTENTS.

CHAPTER I.

THE RELIGION OF THE SON OF MAN.

Evidences of Christianity. — Paley's position. — Miracles. — Prophecy. — Recent objections. — Christianity and Civilization. — Revelation. — What is originality? — Eclecticism. — The relation of the ethnic religions to Christ's religion 13

CHAPTER II.

VEDAISM.

Periods in Indian History. — The Vedas. — The gods. — Kathenotheism. — Asura. — Universality of the Divine. — Kindness of the gods. — Christ's justification of Vedaism. — Weakness of Vedaism 27

CHAPTER III.

BRAHMANISM.

Rise of caste. — New Vedas. — Brahmanas. — Laws of Manu. — Ritual. — Upanishads. — Sât. — Âtman. — Brahma. — Brahmanism and the gospel. — Sacrifice divine. — Need of atonement. — Fatal weakness of Brahmanism 57

CHAPTER IV.

TRANSITION FROM BRAHMANISM TO BUDDHISM.

Mimansa. — Nyaya. — Kapila. — Vedanta. — Lessons of religious history 93

CHAPTER V.

BUDDHISM.

Divisions of Buddhism. — Life of the Buddha. — The great renunciation. — Buddha's teaching. — The existence of pain. — Cause of sorrow. — "The Way." — The Skandhas. — Kamma. — Faith. — Intelligence. — Nirvâna. — Secret of Buddhism 103

CHAPTER VI.

CHRIST'S RELIGION AND BUDDHISM.

Kindred legends in both. — Christian and Buddhist morality, caste, almsgiving, forgiveness of injuries. — Saint and missionary. — Buddhist philosophy and Christian theology. — Sorrow. — The Skandhas and the Incarnation. — Christ's revelation of personality. — Kamma and the cross of Christ. — The power of faith. — Nirvâna and the Christian Heaven. — Buddhist pessimism and Christian hope. — Progress dependent upon knowledge of God 145

CHAPTER VII.

HINDUISM.

Indian Theism. — Return to the Vedas. — The Maha-Bharata. — Shiva. — Shaivism. — Vishnu. — Vaishnuism. — Avatâra. — The Incarnation 178

CHAPTER VIII.

ZOROASTRIANISM.

The Parsis. — The Zend-Avesta. — Bactria. — The first religious schism. — Zoroaster. — Prayer. — Inspiration. — The gods. — Truth and purity. — Moral struggle. — Relation of Zoroastrianism to Judaism. — The Medes. — Fall of Nineveh. — The Captivity. — Cyrus. — Influence of Persian thought. — The Synagogue. — Personal responsibility. — Inspired writings. — Dualism. — Influence on Christian thought. — The absent God. — Importance of purity. — The Resurrection 201

CHAPTER IX.

"THE PERVERSION OF THE GOSPEL."

Review. — The Catholic Church a new thought. — Why is not the world Christian? — Influence of the Roman Empire. — Incursion of the barbarians. — Mediævalism. — The Reformation. — Dogmatism. — Institutionalism. — Sectarianism. — Unity. — Saint Paul the ideal missionary. — Power of sympathy 243

CHAPTER X.

THE FUTURE OF CHRIST'S RELIGION.

Influence of physical science. — Science of comparative religions. — Failure of Christian nations to realize their calling. — Future of humanity. — The evolution of morality. — From what to what? — Humanitarian morality. — Need of hope. — The real dangers. — The lesson of history. — The Brahmo Somaj. — Wise men in the East 267

HIS STAR IN THE EAST.

CHAPTER I.

THE RELIGION OF THE SON OF MAN.

THE purpose of this short study in the early Aryan religions is to call attention to the witness that they bear to man's need of the gospel, and to show that that need has been answered, just in so far as any people, or rather any individual, was prepared to receive it. The assumption that the heathen once had a perfect revelation which they deliberately rejected is far more likely to "cut the nerve of missions" than any theory of the mercy which "endureth forever;" while the belief that God has neglected the larger part of his children will justify men in neglecting them too. But such a position, if once taken by the Church, would lead to a theory of Election, which must harden into a Phariseeism, which is the "middle wall" which Christ came to break down.

The title of the book expresses the thought with which this study began and which subsequent research has deepened, that the "Light which lighteth every man that cometh into the world" has been seen in the East, and that the true way to make disciples of all nations is by declaring unto them Jesus as Agni, Brahma, Buddha, or Sosios, as He was first declared to the Jew as *the Christ*. So considered, the religions of the world become the great " Evidences of Christianity," that is, of Christ.

That there is need of such study seems evident enough; for whatever may have been the merits of the old standards in this department, their usefulness is a thing of the past. That exceedingly interesting book, "The Evidences of Christianity," by Paley, would hardly be referred to to-day in an argument with a skeptic. And the reason is simple enough: Paley's book was written to refute the popular objection of his day, that Christianity was the invention of priests. "No," said Paley, impostors could not work miracles; the disciples worked miracles and thereby proved that what they said was true. Jesus worked miracles and thereby proved that He came from God. Ergo, Christianity was not an invention of impostors. We can scarcely refrain from smiling at the *naïveté* of his argument, yet it was sufficient for such an absurd objection. But it is unfortunate that the argument was ever used against any opponents save those against whom the sturdy Archdeacon aimed it; for it has no force as against men who feel, with Hume, that a miracle is intrinsically so improbable that no evidence is sufficient to prove it.

A second argument — what might be called the intellectual miracle, as opposed to the physical miracles — was found in the literal fulfillment of ancient prophecies in the events recorded in the Gospels. But the new science of Biblical criticism has shown that there is no such literal agreement as we fondly supposed.

Higher ground was taken by the great Bishop Butler, when he said that the proof of the truth of the gospel was found in the willingness of the Apostles to die in the assertion that what is there recorded is true. But we know now that SS. Peter and Paul were both dead before the Gospels were written, and that there is no proof that any Apostle died asserting the truth of the gospel record. And even if it be said that when the " gospel " is spoken of the great saving truths, and not the record, is meant, the answer has been that, even so, the death of, any witness only proves *his* belief in that which he asseverates. And therein lay the weakness of all this great theologian's argument in the second part of the " Analogy." He was influenced by the atmosphere in which he wrote. It was a time when Christianity was spoken of as a "system," — something finished long ago and sent into the world, in which men ought to express a "belief" as the result of a careful weighing of probabilities, with a careful eye to the result in case of error. Such a good man as Dr. Johnson, for instance, was forever talking about Christianity, as we might talk about the pyramids, — as something that existed outside of England, in which he believed because a traveler in whom he had confidence told him that he had seen it! And that was the more remarkable in his case, for he had heard Wesley proclaim the presence of the unseen

King, of the God who had revealed his son in *him*, and caused the light of the gospel to shine in his heart. Methodism was the inevitable reaction from the deism within and without the Church. Its immense superiority to what preceded it is now acknowledged by all; the advances from the position of Paley are not so readily acknowledged, but they are no less great. Hume's dictum concerning miracles has done nothing to discredit the miraculous, but it has made it necessary to think of miracles as the natural effects of a supernatural character, rather than as a proof of a divine mission. And when we say that, we mean that Jesus is known to be the Christ, not after having been kept standing in the antechamber while his credentials were examined, but by the majesty to which all that is worthy in humanity bends the knee.

The new thought about prophecy is nothing less than the recovery of the higher ground on which the Apostle stood who wrote, "the testimony of Jesus is the *spirit* of prophecy." The presence of the prophetic spirit in us is the bond of sympathy by which we are able to recognize the outlines of the ideal man of whom each prophet drew some feature, until we find them all fulfilled and transfigured in the character of the Son of man.

For Paley and Butler and other great and good men to write in answer to the objections of their day was to do a work for which the Church can never be too grateful, but for us to use such arguments to-day is a mark of skepticism. It is as if a man were to say Michael Angelo *did* succeed in making the dome of

St. Peter's float in the liquid air, and yet all the time was building a scaffolding outside it to keep it from falling down. It does float, or it does n't. If it does, it will assert its origin from genius; and if it does not, both it and the scaffolding will fall.

And that is why the old text-books are no longer useful; we have come to feel that the effort to prove Christianity divine is like an effort to prove the virtue of one's mother. A man believes himself to be the son of his reputed father, but in the nature of the case *proof* is impossible. The truth and love and purity and goodness that are forever associated with his mother's character make any other supposition impossible. And so it is that "Evidences of Christianity," as the word is popularly understood, are impossible; for Christianity is only a scholastic term for that which Jesus called the Kingdom of God, which He said was within us, that is, the Christ spirit. The man who has the assurance of the spirit knows that it came forth from God, and the man who has it not cannot be convinced by argument. But *illustrations* of its power and deep meaning will be found in every age and in each individual in which it has been felt. This spirit is like what we call the vital force of nature. Proofs of vegetable life having once existed in the Arctic regions may be found in the fossil remains of plants and flowers. No *proof* of this force is needed in the tropics, yet illustrations of its myriad fantastic forms may be found year after year, and viewed with new interest by all lovers of nature. And so it is with the living power of Christianity. If we would know what form it took in the historic life of Jesus, we may study the Gospels. If we wish to see its power working in the lives of the Apostles, we have the Acts and the Epistles; but if we wish to see how it works to-day, we must look to the life of General Gordon, a free man in his desert prison; to the heroism of our own countrymen, who in the long arctic night had light in all their dwellings, and in their hunger were fed with the bread of life; to the patience of those whom Keble called the "pillars of the Church," the poor, who in garret and in cellar are waiting for the descent of the heavenly city. It is with such illustrations — or evidences — that the Christian pulpit is dealing week after week; but something more seems to be needed, and to that I have ventured to apply myself.

There are two popular objections urged against Christianity, neither of them inspired by a hatred of it, but rather the expression of a feeling that it — a thing which has done and may do good in the world — is hindered by the extravagant claims of its ignorant disciples. The first of these objections is against that claim which asserts that modern civilization is the result of the preaching of the freedom of the sons of God. "Modern civilization," it is said, "is a mighty power, which would have been essentially what it is without the religion of Christ. It would have evolved a religion had not that of the Galilean been at hand convenient for the purpose." This objection was considered a few years since by that distinguished orator, Dr. Richard Storrs, when he held great multitudes of people spellbound by the magic of his rhetoric, and drew a picture of society in Greece and Rome before the coming of Christ,[1] — which if to some it appeared in somewhat darker colors than could be always verified, was still dark enough to show what another century must have brought forth; and then turned to the world of to-day, — which, if far from realizing the seer's vision of the Heavenly Jerusalem, still shows the influence of the new spirit which came with Jesus Christ.

The second objection deals with the origin of Christianity. "Christianity," it is said, "can no longer claim to be a revelation, for there is no such thing as revelation. Every nation has evolved a religion colored by the circumstances by which the nation was surrounded. Nor is that all; Christianity must now forego even its claim to *originality*, for all students of the ethnic religions know that Christianity is a system of eclecticism, the fragments of which may be found scattered from the Yellow Sea to the steppes of Tartary, from the Himalayas to the Nile."[2]

Now to the first objection, that there is no such thing as revealed religion, it is sufficient to answer that all *religion* wherever it may be found, with whomsoever associated, is revealed. Religion, the binding of the soul of man to the Spirit of God, whether we find the fruit of it in the pure contemplation of Confucius, or the sweet mysticism of

---

[1] *The Divine Origin of Christianity indicated by its Historical Defects.* By Richard S. Storrs, D. D., LL. D.

[2] *Evolution and Christianity*, by Yorke.

Buddha, or the wrapt vision of Isaiah, is the same, coming, like "every good and perfect gift, from above." "It is born not of flesh, nor of the will of man, but of God." *But that religion we speak of as most fully revealed, which most perfectly reveals* — a religion which brings to man such a vision of God's character as to change his relation to God, to man, to nature, to life and to time, satisfying and fulfilling what the human consciousness has witnessed to as the fundamental instincts of the human heart, — such a religion so exceeds all others in the *degree* of its revelation as almost to justify us in speaking of it as different in kind, as the only revealed religion. That this is the religion of Jesus we assume. It may be that a serious study of some of the great religions of the world will show that assumption to be one which no thoughtful man need be ashamed to confess.

The other objection, that Christianity lacks originality, has had perhaps greater influence than any objection urged in our day. When it has once been asserted it seems so easy to find illustration of it, it seems so in harmony with the great law of development, that few ask themselves if the supposed illustrations throw light on the subject, and fewer still if the law of evolution does not show that when an original type appears other types begin to disappear. When the new type *man* appeared, many old types ceased to exist, and all evolution of new physical types ceased, and man showed himself a creature linked to the past, and yet having that which the past had never seen, the power to superintend his own future development and modify it in accordance with his own sense of the fitness of things. In other words, man came on the stage of life as a creator.[1]

We start with a like assumption (which it is not the province of this book to prove), — that the religion of the Son of man, while it has its roots in the past religious consciousness of men — specially of Israel — has also an element in it which the past cannot explain.

But what, after all, is originality? Surely it is something more than a question of chronology, otherwise Shakespeare can lay no claim to it. For the plots of a large part of his plays were drawn from Italian originals which had passed through the medium of the French romances, of the sixteenth century, or from older English plays; yet no one will deny that in the truest sense of the term, the "Merchant of Venice," "Othello," and "Hamlet" are original plays. And the reason is this: the test of originality is not to be found so much in the *origin* of a work, if one may so say, as in the *original effect* produced. An old truth set in a new light, or shown to belong to some deeper principle, is as truly original as the first enunciation of it is an isolated fact.

Those who assert that Christianity is a system of eclecticism have not considered, I venture to say, either what eclecticism is or what its effect is.

Cousin's "Lectures on Modern Philosophy," for instance, are an example of eclecticism. "Material-

---

[1] See *The Destiny of Man*, by John Fiske.

ism, Idealism, Mysticism, and Skepticism, these are the four forms that philosophy is perpetually taking," says this delighful lecturer. "There is truth in each; combine those truths and you have the ultimate philosophy." Well, we ask after reading him, what is the central truth into which these partial truths are to fit? And the answer is, "the philosophic spirit of eclecticism." But that is no truth at all. It is simply a state of mind, and what is more, a state of mind that is destined to react against itself into the narrowest dogmatism.

Again, eclecticism is only fitted to produce men "sicklied o'er with the pale cast of thought." It could never have produced a Paul. Now apply either of these tests to the religion of Christ and they will fail. Jesus had no such knowledge of the religious systems of the world as to deliberately form an eclectic system. "True," say our objectors, "but Palestine was full of every sort of doctrine. Buddhist monks and Parsee priests, Egyptian magicians and Hebrew rabbis met in Alexandria, and Antioch, and probably in Jerusalem. It was impossible that Jesus should not have been unconsciously, and his later disciples consciously, influenced by these conflicting doctrines. The morality of the Sermon on the Mount had been preached by Confucius and Buddha, and the so-called 'Lord's Prayer' is a compilation from rabbinic sources." Now in regard to the relation of Christian to Buddhistic morality we shall speak in another chapter; suffice it to say here that the originality of Christ's morality is not to be sought for in any enunciation of a new duty, so much as in the concentration of all duty into the passion of love. And the object of that love is to be found not in an abstract principle, but in the living God, whose character is essentially like that of Jesus; and in our fellow-man made like Jesus and so like God. Jesus revealed sin, not as indulgence in pleasure, nor the violation of a written code, but as the ungrateful violation of the sweet reasonableness of human nature in which God our Father is well pleased.

Jesus satisfies, then, the first test of originality by revealing one fundamental principle into which the morality of humanity can fit.

He satisfies also the second test. He has placed old truths in such a new light that they are essentially new. Thus, take but one petition of the Lord's Prayer. What did " Our Father, who art in Heaven," mean on the lips of the rabbis? It meant a Being who dwelt above the visible vault of heaven, caring for that remnant of the seed of Abraham which kept the ceremonial law as expounded by the scribes. But on the lips of the Christian, it means, in the light of the Incarnation, the Spirit in whom we live and move and have our being, who dwells in the heaven of purity and peace and joy which is "about our path and about our bed," and who creates and guides and loves every child of man who is born into the world. That is the originality of Jesus. Such an illumination of the original instincts of man's spiritual nature as to enable him to take out of his treasures old things, and behold, they become new! The relation which his teaching, or rather his revelation of himself, bore to the teachings of other men was like the relation of the ocean to the streams which irresistibly flow into it. Each little stream and rivulet, each mighty river and placid bay, brings its own force; each inlet has its own eddy; but they do not make the ocean. It absorbs them all and then flows back, filling them with new life and power. So is it with the religion of the Christ. It sweeps by the turbid rivers and vast bays of heathenism and claims kinship with them, fulfilling and purifying them.

Has its effect on life been original, or not? That question has, as has been already said, been well answered by the distinguished divine to whose work we referred. The object of this book is quite different. It is hoped to show by this study that evidences of Christianity, or rather, illustrations of the truth of Christianity, are to be found in the great ethnic religions.

How can that be best done? How can Christianity be proved to be the catholic, the universal religion? for if that can be done, if it can be shown that the religion of Christ contains the desire of humanity, as manifested in the religions of the world, our task will have been completed.

Let us take an illustration that may make our purpose clearer. Suppose a farm of many fields: suppose there be one field that we believe to be all that can be desired; suppose it be objected that each field of the farm has its own advantages, how could we prove the chosen one to be the best? We might begin by pointing out deep buried rocks in one, undestroyed stumps in another, a third might be declared too marshy to produce a crop, — and so we might make the round of the farm, and prove the first field best by comparing its advantages with the disadvantages of all the others. This method is one that seems to commend itself to some who think they are the defenders of the faith. It is, alas! the prevailing note in most meetings held to advocate missions, and perhaps it is the most effective for getting *money — once;* but it must not be used too often; there is a point beyond which faithful Christian people will not go, and where the voice of the scoffer will be heard. "Why try to prove the love of God," it will be said, "to nations whom, on your own showing, God has left from the creation until now in darkness?" Is it not time that the orthodoxy which would magnify the moral grandeur of the ethnic religion of Moses and the Catholic religion of Jesus by depressing the religions of India, China, and Egypt, be declared heresy against the written as well as the unwritten gospel? Surely there must be another way, and — to return to our illustration of the farm — if we began by pointing out the *excellence* of each field in turn, and then showed the *same* excellence in the first, the first field would have been shown to be supremely superior to any of the others in *degree;* but if in addition it could be shown that the first field had anything more than all the others, then its excellence would have been shown to be different in *kind.* This, then, is what it is hoped this book will do: first, point out the excellence of each religion which is considered, and then show that the religion of Christ has the same; secondly, to show that over and above the excellent things which may be found elsewhere, there is that in the gospel which "eye saw not, and ear heard not, and which entered not into the heart of man," but which God hath revealed in the life of Jesus the Christ.

The religions considered here are those in which that branch of the human family known as the Aryan lived and died. Strictly speaking, the Aryan religions include those of India and Persia before the Mohammedan conquest, Greek, Roman, and Teutonic mythologies. But this book will treat only of the religions of India, or what may be called the early Aryan.

CHAPTER II.

VEDAISM.

The religious history of India divides itself into four periods, viz.: I. The Vedic; II. The Brahmanic; III. The Buddhist; and IV. The Hindu.

The Vedic cannot easily be separated from the Brahmanic, because the one flowed by an unbroken gradation into the other. But it has been said that the difference between the two periods is this: " The Vedic age was the one in which the main traditions of the Maha-Bharata and Ramayana seem to have taken place; whilst the Brahmanic age, which succeeded to the Vedic period, was the one in which the two poems were composed."[1] The Maha-Bharata, or "Great War of the Bharata," has for its foundation the struggle of the two rival branches of the great Bharata family,—a sort of Indian "War of the Roses," which took place in that part of India lying north of Allahabad and east of the Punjab. This was probably about a thousand years before our era,—some would place it as early as fifteen hundred years before.

The traditions of this struggle were to the descendants of the mighty Bharata what the siege of Troy was to the Greeks: and having been sung by

[1] *History of India*, by J. Talboys Wheeler, vol. i.

the minstrels and recounted by the story-tellers, they took permanent form in the great Indian Epic, under the hands of the Brahmans, who made it the vehicle of theological instruction.[1] Of its theological bias we shall have occasion to speak later; now we have need only to note what it has to teach us of the habits of the people of whom it speaks.

But of course the great storehouse from which we must draw our materials is the Rig-Veda. The Vedas or "knowledge," the sacred writings of the Vedic-Aryans, are probably the oldest of all the efforts made by man to record the influence of God's spirit upon his soul. The Hindus believe that the original Veda was written by Brahma, and that having been preserved by tradition, it was finally arranged in its present form by the sage Dwaipayana, or Vyasa, — the "collector," as he is commonly called. These Vedas are divided into four parts, of which the first, called the Rich or Veda in *metre*, has given the name Rig-Veda to the whole collection.[2] But the Rig-Veda proper is the only one which is undoubtedly "Vedic," the other three are Brahmanic.

The whole chronology of India is too uncertain, too much like objects seen in a dream, to enable us to determine with any certainty the date of the Rig-Veda, but it is probable that the last of the hymns had been written before the great war, for the sailors of Solomon who brought back the treasures of the Indies to Jerusalem used the names which were given in India, but which were no longer the pure

---

[1] Colebrooke's *Misc. Essays*, vol. i.
[2] *History of India*, J. Talboys Wheeler, vol. i.

forms of the Rig-Veda;[1] so that if its language was archaic in the time of Solomon, it is allowing none too much time, in that age of slow change, if we say that the last of the hymns had been sung before Moses led the people out of Egypt.

Out of the mystery which shrouds the table-land of Central Asia, into the land of the Five Rivers, came the fathers of the Indo-Aryan race. They were a company of herdsmen, and the prayer which was ever on their lips was that the heavens would give them rain; for unless the clouds, the "heavenly kine," let down their udders, the earthly cattle must die. That is the way their religious sense first expressed itself; rising from the immediate human want, in prayer to the infinitely human power which could sympathize with man, and be touched with the feeling of his infirmities. To the God, then, who had power over sun and rain, to the God of the firmament, the most frequent prayer was addressed.

The chanters extol Indra with sòngs.

Indra, the blender of all things, comes verily with his steeds that are harnessed at his word; Indra, the richly decorated, the wielder of the thunderbolt.

Indra, to render all things visible, elevated the sun in the sky, and charged the cloud with abundant waters.

Shedder of rain, granter of all desires, set open this cloud. Thou art never uncompliant with our requests.

The shedder of rain, the mighty lord, the always compliant, invests men with his strength, as a bull defends a herd of kine.[2]

[1] Stanley's *Jewish History*, second series.
[2] *Rig-Veda Sanhita*, Wilson, vol. i. p. 18.

But still Indra was far away, and it might be that prayer, though it were chanted with frequent cry, would not pierce the vaulted sky. What had man that could pass from himself to Indra? The only thing was fire. But that too must be divine. How else could it enter the heavenly tents? And it *was* divine, for it came out of mystery to the dwellings of men. Agni, then, would be the mediator between man and God. And so they sang: —

We select Agni, the messenger of the gods, their invoker, the possessor of riches, the perfecter of this rite.

Agni, generated by attrition, bring hither the gods to the clipt grass; thou art their invoker for us, and art to be adored.

As thou dischargest the duty of messenger, arouse them desirous of the oblation; sit down with them on the sacred grass.

Agni, the bright, the purifier! bring hither the gods to our sacrifice, to our oblations.

Agni, shining with pure radiance, and charged with all the invocations of the gods, be pleased with this our praise.[1]

When the gods should come they would give them the best they had; that which was most likely to please them, as it pleased men, the inspiring Soma juice.

Indra, let thy coursers hither bring thee, bestower of desires, to drink the Soma juice; may the priests, radiant as the sun, make thee manifest.

We invoke Indra at the morning rite, we invoke him at the succeeding sacrifice, we invoke Indra to drink the Soma juice.

[1] *Rig-Veda Sanhita*, vol. i. p. 29.

These dripping Soma juices are effused upon the sacred grass; drink them, Indra, to recruit thy vigor.

May this our excellent hymn, touching thy heart, be grateful to thee, and thence drink the effused libation.[1]

By the same process of thought which we have noted in the case of Agni, Soma, first thought of as a gift acceptable to the gods, became later a god himself.

Thou, Soma, art thoroughly apprehended by our understanding; thou leadest us along a straight path; by thy guidance, our righteous fathers obtained wealth among the gods.

Thou, Soma, art the protector, the sovereign of the pious, ... thou art holy sacrifice. Thou, Soma, hast generated all these herbs, the water, the kine; thou hast spread out the spacious firmament; thou hast scattered darkness with light.

Divine and potent Soma, bestow upon us with thy brilliant mind, a portion of wealth.[2]

Thus the religion began. There was no ritual but the family meal, in which the gods were asked to share. The newly cut grass was arranged in a ring for the gods to sit on. There was no priest save the father of the household; his sons were the assistants, and the family was the congregation.

A favorable spot having been chosen, the fire was lighted at sunrise, and a hymn, sometimes homely in its simple expression of trust, sometimes sublime in the effort of the human spirit to speak with the inspirer and hearer of prayer, and always pathetic in its yearning, was chanted by the father and his sons. Add to this ceremony of the chanted hymn

---

[1] *Rig-Veda*, vol. i. p. 39.
[2] Ibid. vol. i. p. 232.

and the lighted fire, the pouring out of the clarified butter of the humble household and the sprinkling of the Soma juice, and we have a picture of the Vedic ritual before it had been elaborated by Brahmanic hands. Though, as we have seen, Indra, Agni, and Soma were the earliest gods of the Vedic pantheon, yet the hymns, as we find them now, were addressed impartially to all the great phenomena of nature.

Indra, the ruler of the sky, he who in his power held back the chariot of the sun as it descended the western slope, he who refreshed the thirsty earth, he at first was God of gods. When the storm gathered on the mountain tops and came hurtling into the valley below, bending the pines, scattering the cattle, blasting the mighty tree that dared to lift up its head, they said that Rudra, the great storm king, shot forth his thunderbolts.

But it was not only in the active forces of nature that men found the witnesses to the divine presence.

There are long days in India when the stillness of life under the burning sun is indescribable. Above, below, and on every side the great tide of sunlight fills all space. Such was not a day of Indra, for Indra was the personification of the active forces of the atmosphere, and now all things hang in heaven still. Not a day of Rudra, for no thunderbolt could pierce that vault of blue. Not a day of Agni, either, for the fire on the hearth is not needed when all is fire. On such a day the Vedas praised Varuna, the Greek Οὐρανός; the still, serene, and glorious heaven. In the cloudless sky, full of unseen power, the Aryan found the fittest symbol of the peaceful goodness of the gods; and so we find the noblest hymns addressed to Varuna, and to him ascended, too, the most frequent cry for pardon.

However we break from thy laws from day to day, men as we are, O god Varuna,

Do not deliver us unto death, nor to the blow of the furious, nor to the wrath of the spiteful!

To propitiate thee, O Varuna, we unbend thy mind with songs, as the charioteer a weary steed.

He who knows the place of the birds that fly through the sky, who on the waters knows the ships; —

He, the upholder of order, he who knows the twelve months with the offspring of each, and knows the month that is engendered afterwards; —

He who knows the track of the wind, of the wide, the bright, the mighty; and knows those who reside on high; —

He the upholder of order, Varuna, sits down among his people; he the wise sits there to govern.

May he, the wise Aditya, make our paths straight all our days; may he prolong our lives!

Yearning for him, the far-seeing, my thoughts move onward, as kine move to their pastures.

O hear this, my calling, Varuna, be gracious now; longing for help, I have called upon thee.

Thou, O wise god, art lord of all, of heaven and earth: listen on thy way.[1]

The god whose light filled every crevice, whose presence quickened the limbs of the old, and whose warm breath drew forth the reptile and beast to bask in his glory, who lifted the humble fern on high and changed it to a tree of the forest, — surely he was

---

[1] Max Müller's Lectures on the Vedas, *Chips from a German Workshop*, vol. i.

the god who could not be deceived; he must mean well to all life; he had power to lift up the troubled soul.

But there was a unity which underlay this seeming diversity. The earliest of the hymns indicate that this mysterious unity was concealed in the joint action of the two deities Agni and Soma. For while Agni was fire and Soma was the juice of the plant, yet they were at the same time the source of life and activity. We have seen how Agni manifested itself in many ways, but there were manifestations back of those, so to speak. Agni, before it appeared on the hearth as fire, had lain hid in the " womb of the wood," which by friction had brought forth.[1] So that Agni was without beginning and also without end. For when *he* issued forth into the flashing thunderbolt or reigned supreme in the cloudless sky, *he* had passed beyond the ken of mortals.

There is something at once sublime and pathetic in this belief in the eternity of the original element, together with the clinging to the hope of its manifestation in the common life of man. It is the first intimation, as far as I know, of that irrepressible yearning of the human soul for an incarnation of the divine.

The other indestructible element was Soma. That also had a material side which was never lost sight of; but it too went forth into the immensity of life where the eye of man could no longer follow it. As it quickened the pulses of men, it came to be thought

---

[1] "Agni, generated by attrition." — *Rig-Veda*, vol. i. p. 29.

of as the originator of life. It gave the power to the plant to grow, to women to conceive, to the cow to secrete milk ; in fine, it was the origin of all the forces of secret growth, as Agni was of the active, manifesting powers of life.

Thus was begun that system of the transmigration of an eternal principle which is the key to all the theology of India. Whatever we may call the special modifying philosophical beliefs which came in later, they all centre in this faith. There is an eternal principle which folds and unfolds itself ceaselessly in the manifold appearances of life. It took tremendous proportions in later ages, but at the time we are now considering it was as simple as possible.

This lurking duality of Agni and Soma, which seems to have been the first effort toward unity, soon issued into a sort of monotheism, which found expression in the name BRAHMANASPATI, the Father of the Gods. And in order to approach this divine life there was need of more than ritual, there was need of faith. Thus we read, " He *who with a believing mind* worships Brahmanaspati, the father of the gods, with oblations, he verily receives food, together with his sons, his kindred, his descendants, and obtains riches with all men." [1]

This necessity for faith is indicated again : " Excite in us, Indra, veneration for the sun, for the waters, and for those who are worthy of the praise of living beings, as exempt from sin ; injure not our offspring while yet in the womb, *for our trust is* in thy mighty power." [2]

---

[1] *Rig-Veda Sanhita*, trans. by Wilson, vol. ii. p. 273.
[2] Ibid. vol. i. p. 269.

It was formerly supposed that sacrifices formed no part of the Vedic ritual; that they were the result of the later philosophy, which we call Brahmanic, but this is now known to be a mistake. That sacrifices did not take the proportions at first which they afterwards assumed is true; but the necessity for sacrifices is indicated in the earliest of the hymns, not as a means of expiating sin, but as a means of sustaining the gods. This conception of sacrifice, so different from the common " heathen " view, and so entirely opposed to the later Hebrew belief, was the natural outcome of that fundamental conception of the Hindu mind already mentioned. So firmly were the authors of the Vedic hymns convinced that all things issued from the source to which they must return, that they believed that the gods were dependent upon men as truly as men were dependent upon the gods![1]

Undoubtedly that idea of sacrifice sunk later to the common heathen notion of propitiation, but originally it was the result of the belief in the mutual dependence of each life upon all other life. And therefore they said, with a divine insight that has been too little noted, that creation was accompanied by sacrifice. Around the unbroken ring of existence all energy must return upon itself. The fire on the hearth, the heavenly fires in their courses, the flashing thunderbolt, — they were all different, and yet they were one.

What shall we say of these people? Were they monotheistic, or polytheistic? It seems difficult to

[1] *The Religions of India*, by A. Barth, trans. by Rev. J. Wood.

affirm either. They were not monotheistic, because under the manifold manifestations of the divine they did not grasp the idea of one personal character. Nor were they polytheistic, for they seemed in worshiping Indra to ignore Agni and to have forgotten Varuna, and so each in turn was made supreme, and the others did not appear above the horizon of consciousness.[1]

We have mentioned the more prominent of the gods, or rather names of the divine essence, but there were many others, as again and again men tried to speak a name which would more perfectly express the divine character which was being made manifest to them through the experiences of life. Sometimes it was the activity of a man, sometimes it was the strength of a brute, again it was the unselfish forth-giving of the vegetable life, which seemed best to symbolize the power, or the goodness, or the wisdom of the divine.

Little by little the old names of which we have spoken began to be felt by the subtler thinkers to be insufficient as expressions of the divine life, and instead of the rising sun, and the flashing thunderbolt, and the upleaping flame, the Rishis[2] began to speak of a neuter principle of life manifesting itself in a glorious body. Life, and birth, and death, and change, what are they? The rushing wind causing

[1] "This is not surely what we understand by polytheism. Yet it would be equally wrong to call it monotheism. I should call it Kathenotheism." — Max Müller, *Chips from a German Workshop*, vol. i. p. 28.
[2] The priests.

the great trees to moan and rock, the sudden calm, whence came they? Some day the air is full of perfume, the pines are sending out their incense as the warm sun kisses them. A fire is started in the forest, it sweeps for miles in its destructive course and then stops. How came these things to be so? The Vedic-Aryans said it was Asura. The glorious body of the unseen god, changing at every instant, was what we call life and death; the blowing of the wind was the breath of his nostrils; the unseen perfume was the sign of his presence; the raging of the fire was the fury of "the glorious body of the principle of life, which is for itself and for others the origin of movement."[1] They had tried by the doctrine of Asura to bring the divine near to them, and behold they had placed it beneath them! Yet their experience was not a unique one; they were impressed with the phenomena of nature, they were sure that they witnessed to a higher life than their own, they could not tell which of these phenomena was supreme, so each became supreme in turn. It was not the rigid purity of the monotheist, but it was far from the licentious excess of the polytheist. It was the first attempt of the human mind to realize the universality of the divine; wherever the child placed its hand it felt the thrill of divine life. *Nothing without God*, that was the discovery — if one likes the word — of the early Aryan mind. That was the revelation, I should prefer to say, of the everlasting Father to his children, amidst the glorious scenery of India. Illustrations of this truth

[1] *Essai sur le Véda*, par E. Burnouf, pp. 320–340.

abound in the Rig-Veda. Thus, "Aditi, *i. e.*, 'the Absolute,' is heaven. Aditi is the firmament. Aditi is father, mother, son. Aditi is all the gods."[1] Again:—

Thou art the supreme God, the eternal, celestial spirit, that all the Rishis confess. That also thou dost announce thyself to me. I believe in the truth of thy word, but I know not how to render thee visible to me. Thou thyself alone dost know thyself, Being of beings, God of gods, Lord of all creatures. . . . It is in thee that we are; I and all those beings which surround me. . . . I see in thy unity all the universe, with all things visible and invisible. Thou dost burn like the fire and like the sun in thy immensity, mountain of light, on all sides resplendent, without commencement, without middle, without end.[2]

This revelation the Vedic Aryans were led into much as the Hebrews were led. God's message to the Aryan was read in the blazing sunlight, was heard in the awful muttering of the storm, was felt when the gigantic pines bent and bowed themselves as He drew near. But the message to Israel came through the experiences of a nation. Not through nature, but through man. Yet see how long they were in learning it! That which now seems to us so plain, that there is but one God, the Hebrews at the beginning would not have understood. At first they spoke of the God of Abraham and of Isaac and of Jacob, they did not doubt that there were other gods. They asked Pharaoh to let them go that they

---

[1] *Rig-Veda Sanhita*, trans. by Wilson, vol. i. p. 230.
[2] *Essai sur le Véda*, par E. Burnouf, p. 307.

might worship *their* God. Later they became bolder, and said there is no God like our God, "He shall be our guide unto death." While the "God of Jacob" was with them they would not fear. Not till the time of Isaiah could they say, "There is no God but the Lord." What the Hebrew asserted of the spiritual forces of life, the Aryan had said of the phenomena of nature. The Hebrews were led to believe in the one God by seeing the superiority of the idea of the God of Israel, over those ideas which held sway among the heathen about them. The unity of the divine was the revelation to the Hebrew, the universality of the divine was the revelation to the Aryan.

But this is not the only way in which the Rig-Veda reminds us of the Bible. The most careless reader of these hymns cannot fail to be struck with the absence of anything like fear of the gods. It is a tone of childlike confidence that sounds throughout. Now when we remember that these are the oldest of all religious books, we shall be inclined to doubt the popular belief that all religion begins in fear. If fetichism be the earliest manifestation of human fear of something beyond the seen, still that can hardly be called religion, for religion means the conscious relation to the unseen. It is true that the fear of the gods seems to be the most powerful element in the debased heathen worship with which the traveler comes in contact to-day, but it was not always so, as Aryan and Semitic history show. At the beginning of Hebrew history stands Abraham and he was called the friend of God; in the childhood of Aryanism were chanted the Vedic hymns, and to these singers the gods seemed very friendly. Again and again they tell the flame to mount up quickly, and from the far-off sky call the gods to the sacrifice, that they with men may drink the inspiring Soma juice and rejoice. And yet this sense of friendliness was not the result of moral obtuseness, for there are frequent prayers for deliverance from sin.

I invoke the divine waters: waters, take away whatsoever sin has been formed in me, whether I have knowingly done wrong, or pronounced imprecations against holy men, or have spoken untruth.[1]

Varuna, loosen for me the upper, the middle, the lower band, so, son of Aditi, shall we through righteousness in thy worship become freed from sin.

Preserve him who praises thee from sin with bands of iron.

Dissolve not, Agni, our ancestral friendship, for thou art cognizant of the past as well as of the present: in like manner as light speeds over the sky, so decay impairs my body; think of me before that scene of destruction prevails.[2]

The scope of this inquiry does not lead us to consider the morality of the Vedas except in as far as they give indications of a belief on the part of the

---

[1] *Rig-Veda Sanhita*, Wilson, vol. i. pp. 57, 58, 64, 156, 158.

[2] The most beautiful hymn to Varuna, with the refrain "have mercy, Almighty, have mercy," is so well known that I do not quote it, fearing it may be supposed to be the only one of its kind. It will be found entire in Max Müller's *Chips from a German Workshop*, vol. i., and in Dr. James Freeman Clarke's *Ten Great Religions*.

Vedic-Aryans that the faith expressed in the hymns must be incorporated into life.[1]

When the Vedic-Aryans first appear in the Punjab they are seen to show evidence of a struggle elsewhere. What that was we shall see later, but for the present it is only necessary to bear in mind that there had been a great religious struggle, and that these herdsmen believed themselves to be in the right. So the first prayers which they uttered, prayers which at first sight might seem to show no feeling save that of selfishness, a desire to get as much as possible of this world's goods, are more than that. They pray indeed for rain and food, for prolific cattle, for health and safety from storms, but it is as men who feel that they have a claim on the gods, as those who have " kept the faith " in the midst of a perverse generation.

So the prayer for temporal prosperity is really a plea for justice. " If I, O Indra," says one of the bards, " if I were master of such wealth as thou, I would be generous to him that praised me, but would bestow nothing upon the wicked : day by day would I give in abundance to him who paid me honor, be he who he might. We have no dearer relative than thou, were it a father even."

If it be answered, that this does not show a high standard of morality, the answer is we have no right to demand a high standard at such a stage of experience. It is not found among any people, not even among the most religious the world has ever seen — the Jews.

---

[1] See Roth's " Morality of the Vedas," in *Journal of American Oriental Society*, vol. iii. 1853.

But a better means of judging of their sense of right and wrong is found in noting what they condemn in themselves. Like all nomadic people, the vice of gambling was widespread. Yet we find a hymn in the Rig-Veda in which the gambler bewails his fault, recognizes his sin, and confesses that he finds no means of escape.

The absence of fear, already spoken of as a characteristic of the hymns, would lead us to suspect that there would be a contempt of the power of the gods. But this is far from being the case. The sense of the good-will of the gods to men saved them from thinking of them as powers which might turn on the dead, but this did not lead to licentiousness; they prayed for forgiveness and believed that the wicked should be thrust down into the deep by Varuna, the supreme judge of the living and of the dead. But in the mystery of the darkness that was apart from the presence of the God of the cloudless sky, they left the wicked, and did not exercise their imaginations in an effort to depict the torture of the unhappy dead until all sense of the loving kindness of the celestials had given place to a fear which could only be allayed by bloody sacrifices. That was as far from the thought of the Vedic Aryans, as the worship of Moloch was from the father of the faithful.

But perhaps the belief which had the most healthy moral effect was that fundamental faith in the universality of the divine which may be called the distinguishing mark of the Vedic age. This belief, which on its intellectual side was so perilously near to polytheism, on its moral side was saved from degradation by being ascribed to Varuna, the all-seeing God, as Omniscience. He counts the very " winks of the eyes of men." When two whisper together he hears them, and yet he knows the flight of the bird and the path of the wind.

He whose light can strike into the shadows of the mountain cave, he too can shine into the darkened heart of man and reveal its secrets. That consciousness of the abiding presence of One " to whom all hearts are open, all desires known, and from whom no secrets are hid," [1] is still believed to be the best preventive of immorality, and so was it thought to be by the men who kept their herds on the plains of the Punjab, when Abraham still dwelt in Ur of the Chaldees.

We have now reached a point where we may pause and ask ourselves what are the leading ideas of the Rig-Veda, and what has the religion of Jesus that can affiliate with them. Of course one who does not believe that any common ground can, or ought to be found, will be able to point to much in these hymns which our taste must repudiate and our conscience condemn; but our object is very different; it is to find, if possible, not what is common and gross and immoral in this system, and compare it with the excellences of the religion of Jesus, but rather, believing that every good and perfect gift is from above, to find the good and then show that Christianity can fulfill it as truly as it does the law and the prophets of Israel.

---

[1] See the Prayer at the beginning of the Communion Service, in the Book of Common Prayer.

There are, then, four points to which I would call attention in the Rig-Veda. They are, first, that earliest expression of the religious instinct, the prayer for bread and health and peace. Secondly, the prayer for the divine participation in sacrifice; thirdly, faith in the divine good-will to good men; and, lastly, the belief in the divine universality.

The first is not peculiar to the Vedic-Aryans; it is the prayer that the child-spirit of humanity frames when its eyes first open to the mystery of life. But when Christ came with his revelation of the spirituality of God He did not ignore this great human want. The first prayer that He bade his disciples put up for themselves was that they might receive their daily bread. No doubt the prayer for daily bread in the mouth of Him whose meat and drink it was to do the will of God was far more than any prayer for bodily sustenance, but it included it. The man who knows that man does not live by bread alone will mean something very different from the poor starving child of God, when he says, "Our Father, give me this day my daily bread;" but the same thought underlies the two prayers, and that is faith in One who knows what we have need of before we ask, but to whom we can come in our ignorance, asking for that which it seems to us we need; whether it be food for ourselves or for our children, or house or raiment. When Christ put a prayer in the mouth of his disciples, it was one which would express the deepest cravings of a soul athirst for God, and at the same time reach down and serve as a ladder, by means of which the hungry herdsman might mount to the knowledge of One in whom he lived and moved and had his being. In teaching a prayer which expressed not only the saints' hunger and thirst after Righteousness, but also the primary craving of the natural man, Christ has shown that no religion is outside the range of his sympathy; no nation too far from the divine life to hear the good news that the faith of its fathers has been justified.

Of the second point it is hardly necessary to speak; it is so evident that the prayer for the divine presence is a Christian prayer. Not that I would have it supposed that I think the Rig-Veda is the gospel before Christ, — far from it! I only believe that it was a prophecy of the gospel, and that when that which is perfect had come, that which was in part was to be done away. And this second prayer is an illustration of that. It is true that the Rishis prayed for the divine presence, and so does the Lord's Prayer. "Thy kingdom come" is common to both, but in the Rig-Veda the coming of the kingdom is made dependent upon the giving of bread, and in the Lord's Prayer the giving of bread is made dependent upon the coming of the kingdom! The Vedic-Aryans prayed for bread, and then asked the gods to share it with them, because they believed that the gods themselves were dependent upon the family meal for their own strength. But with Jesus the prayer was for bread, only if it would not prevent the nourishment of his soul with the bread of life. In other words, the Vedic-Aryan believed that the kingdom would come if he was cared for, and the Christian believes that if the kingdom comes he will not be forgotten.

I repeat, the man who does not believe that the Rig-Veda is any revelation of the divine character to men will turn over its pages and find nothing but the weary repetition of extravagant epithets addressed to the Dawn or to the Maruts; a confused mythology, and sometimes gross sensuality, yet the same man might read the revelation to Israel and fail to see the writing of the finger of God! But the traces of it are to be found in both: in one so plain that he who runs may read; and in the other not so obscure that he who would find should fail.

We have spoken of the answer to the Aryan's prayer in the great Christian prayer, nor need we go beyond that to find the justification of their faith that if the divine life came among men it would be favorable to them, and rejoice in their simple joys and mourn with them in the old sorrrow that was no more absent from the valley of the Indus than from the shores of the lake of Galilee. The message of the first Christmas carol was forever perpetuated in the prayer of Jesus. When the divine life came, the tradition embodied in the gospel is that the angels sang "Peace on earth, good-will to men." "When ye pray," said Jesus, "say Our Father. Pray to Him who maketh his sun to rise on the evil and on the good. Pray to Him who so loved the world that he sent his son, not to condemn the world, but that the world by Him might be saved."

And the whole life of Jesus was in harmony with this Aryan faith that when the divine life came to join in the sacrifice it would have good-will to men. He went about doing good, and preaching the good news of the kingdom of God — of God whom He always called the Father. And that word, Father, means the everlasting friend of the human soul, whom neither the darkness of ignorance, nor the cloud of sin, nor the mountain barrier of prejudice can hold back from that communion, which, as the Aryan dimly saw, is the joy of God and the life of man.

It remains now for us to inquire if Christianity has any answer to the yearning of the Aryan soul for the universality of God which expressed itself so insufficiently in the doctrine of Asura.

If we consider Christianity as represented in the life of Jesus, we cannot fail to be struck with the frequency and apparent naturalness of what we call the miraculous. Whatever explanation men may think best to give of it, even should they be led to deny the accuracy of the description of certain events in the life of Jesus, it will still remain in the last analysis a miraculous life; and those special manifestations which we call "miracles" were spoken of, by those who it is asserted witnessed them, as "signs"; were declared by Him who is reported to have worked them to be signs, or manifestations, not of a power within himself, but the manifestations of the power of Him who created all things. Whether these be matters of fact, or stories, or legends of that Life, it is not my purpose to discuss; the point to which I wish to call attention is this: that these stories give the best representation of the way in which Jesus regarded nature; which is the question that concerns us now. The gospel presents us the picture of one full of divine energy going throughout the land and healing those who were diseased; in many cases these diseases were asserted to be the effect of the presence of an evil spirit; in every case they were treated as the effect of some interruption of the divine purpose. Jesus seems to have looked into the life of the man whom he undertook to heal, and to have seen there the contradiction of the power of God. His miracle consisted in the removing of this hostile power, this foreign substance, as the physicians would say to-day. So considered, every miracle was as truly a witness to the presence of the divine life in the diseased body as the physician's administration of medicine is a witness to his belief in the presence and power of the vital force. And just as a physician only pretends to "assist nature," so the miracle of Jesus was the setting free of the current of the divine life which had been checked. The miracles of Jesus are not represented as the result of the exercise of external power so much as the coöperation with the power within nature itself, which was possible only to him who had entered into the secret councils of God. This picture, then, is of one who knew no man in whom there was not a spark of the divine life which might not be blown upon by the gentle breath of sympathy until the flame of love to the father revived; and also of one who knew nothing of a kosmos divorced from God; who saw the divine will and love and wisdom working amid the groaning and travailing of the creation, and coöperating with that divine life immanent in nature, wrought the wonders which have been related of Him, and which seem so incredible to the men who have never found trace of God in the work of his hands. Every miracle of Jesus was bearing witness to the faith of the Aryan, that there is no mountain, no river, no tree, no man, no object, animate or inanimate, in which there is not the presence of God.

But they were doing more than that. Those miracles which are reported of the birth of Jesus, and of his resurrection; those stories of the wonders wrought by Him, not alone upon the bodies of men, but also upon what we call inanimate nature, were bearing witness to the divine presence in all the kosmos, and at the same time to the truth that there is a *difference* in the manifestation of power; that though it be true to speak of God as immanent in nature, it is fatal to belief in the Fatherhood of God to think of Him as contained in nature; for while it be true that manifestations of divine wisdom and love and power may be found in nature, it is only by those who have first found them within man.[1] Jesus gave to mankind the highest manifestation of the divine when he let it shine through his own personality, and in the light of that personality we can see that which He saw, that nature is instinct with the divine presence. So considered, the miracles of Jesus become something more than the justification of the faith of the Aryan in the immanence of the divine life, they be-

---

[1] See "Nature and God," in *Essays, Philosophical and Theological*. By James Martineau, vol. i. New York: Henry Holt & Co.

come a revelation of that which the Aryan failed to grasp, which is *the superiority of the human manifestation of the divine life:* and just because of that lack the Vedic-Aryan was always confused in regard to the relation of man to nature. He could not tell whether the spiritual life of man has its origin in matter or whether matter is an expression of mind. And that confusion became fatal to progress. The history of Hindu thought is a weary round of questioning: Brahmanism pushed idealism to the extreme until matter became the one unreality; and modern Hinduism, rushing to the other pole, reached in its gross idolatry the lowest point of degradation when it ascribed the origin of life to sexual intercourse and worshiped the genital organs, as is done in India to-day. This inability to recognize character as the highest manifestation of divine life lies back of the modern as of the ancient perplexity concerning the origin of matter. When character is recognized as the highest manifestation of life possible, then it becomes a matter of indifference whether or not the material from which the kosmos has been evolved, be thought of as coexistent with God or not. I think it is only in this day that we are entering into that higher conception of God as a creator which the Aryan was feeling after but failed to grasp, but which the miracles of Jesus were revealing. A well-known French writer has declared that the idea of creation is not to be found in the Vedas, but " the universal agent is the productor, the generator of beings, and the father of the living. The supreme and universal Being is not a person separated from the world."[1] But surely he has in mind a notion of creation which we ourselves have found to be inadequate to that larger knowledge of the kosmos into which we have been led. There is no inconsistency in thinking of the Supreme Being as existing apart from nature and yet immanent in nature. If we turn back in thought to that word which Jesus always used of the Supreme — Father, — we shall gain, I believe, a conception of nature truer and far nobler than that which has been contemptuously called the "Carpenter theory." The creation of a father is the forthgiving of a father's life. It has been well said that "the self imparting energy of love is the first cause of creation." The miracles of Jesus showed that this self-imparting energy of love was omnipresent in his day: in other words, that creation was not an accomplished fact, the result of a divine fiat in a moment of time, long ages ago; but rather that it is the constant upholding of nature by God's presence, which makes creation a perpetual act. The fatherhood of God in its relation to nature means the immanence of creative power. Without the knowledge of the correlation of physical forces, St. Paul yet entered into the true spiritual science of nature when he wrote, "In Him we live and move and have our being."

That is the answer of Christianity to the Aryan, who says, "To our fathers was revealed the truth of the Universality, the Omnipresence of the Divine. We can recognize no religion as true which has no place for this fundamental belief of the Vedic-Aryan;

[1] E. Burnouf, *Essai sur le Véda*, p. 453.

for our religious consciousness will bear no clearer witness to any new truth of religion than it does to that old one." We do not need to make little of such a sublime faith; we believe that the gospel of Jesus comprehended it in the larger revelation to mankind. We have only to look back to the life of Jesus, in the new sense of the nearness of God which has come through the study of nature in this day, to see that by Jesus nature was always treated as man was treated, as that which had within itself the divine life.

When He drew near to man, He drew near to the divinity which was in him; and when He drew near to nature, He did so as one who felt that man and nature form one great whole.

The disorders in nature are from a lack of harmony between human reason, which is the manifestation of the divine in man, and force and law, which are the divine manifestation in nature. Jesus never lost sight of and never confused the triple manifestation of the Divine Life. God in Himself; that which no man hath seen nor can see. God in man; God in nature. But just as God in man, the Christ, is subject to God the Father, so God in nature, Force, is to be subject to God in man, Reason. And yet nature is an entity distinct from man, and man is an entity distinct from God. The perfect harmony of thought and life will be possible only when all nature having been subjected unto the Son of man, He himself becomes subjected unto the Father, that God may be all in all.[1]

[1] 1 Cor. xv. 28, R. V.

Now with all this good, with all the noble truths which were incorporated in it, it still ought not be difficult for us to say why Vedaism failed. For it did fail; Brahmanism, which grew from its roots, lived by the power of a new truth which it introduced into the system. Vedaism failed because it was nature worship. Not that the material universe was worshiped, but the Divine Essence was conceived of as dwelling in nature exclusively. The illustrations of divine power were found in the storm; of divine goodness in the refreshing rain; of divine care in the unerring sunrise. Such very likely has been the beginning of every religion, and its influence will be felt just so long as the people continue in intimate contact with nature. So at least it was with the Vedic-Aryan. When the nomadic herdsman life had passed away, and men began to feel in a higher civilization that their welfare depended not so much upon nature as upon man, the old nature worship no longer satisfied and comforted them. The beautiful goodness of nature had given place to the cunning of man, and the gods of the mountains seemed powerless in the village and in the town.

If now it be asked why, in the progress of civilization, the Aryans did not bring their gods down with them from the mountains and enthrone them as village divinities, even as Abraham came into Canaan with the God he had known in Ur of the Chaldees, the answer is that the fundamental error of the Hindu religion lay at the root of Vedaism. That error was Pantheism. God was not a person. In other words there was no God. There was a divine unknown, unseen mystery back of life, which took personal and impersonal forms, but it was not essentially personal; there was no will, nor affection, nor self-consciousness. As therefore there was no divine person, there could be no personal identity between Brahmanism and Vedaism. When the herdsmen of Afghanistan built cities in the valley of the Indus, they left the gods of their fathers behind them and gave to the Divine Essence new names. That Pantheism was the necessary form for the transmission of the truth of the immanence of God, we may believe as firmly as that Anthropomorphism was the necessary illusion for the perpetuation of the belief in the personality of God. In which case the election of the Hebrew, for transmitting the one will be no more apparent than the mission of the Aryan in the preservation of the other. I have tried to show how the gospel of Jesus is full of the idea of the immanence of God. Every reader of the Bible knows how in the teaching of the Master the old anthropomorphic symbol of the Jewish dispensation fell away, and the God in " whom we live and move and have our being," "who is about our path and about our bed," stood revealed as the Father of our Lord Jesus Christ, loving every human soul, governing every wayward child, healing our sicknesses, cleansing our sins, lifting us from the death of sin to the life of righteousness. So, then, if I were asked for an illustration of Christianity as being the revelation in which all the nations of the world are to be blest, I would answer: in the life of Jesus is gathered the Aryan revelation of the Immanence of God, and the Semitic revelation of the Personality of God; and more, in that commingling both are transfigured; the Immanence of God means power and law and wisdom manifesting themselves as making for righteousness; and the Personality of God means love and forgiveness and grace gathering together the children of God that are scattered abroad.

CHAPTER III.

BRAHMANISM.

THE second phase of the religion of India is called Brahmanism. It is not easy to draw a line which shall divide Brahmanism from Vedaism; the former is an outgrowth of the latter. The simple ritual of the Vedas expanded by slow degrees into the elaborate ceremonial of the Brahmanic sacrifices, which were so expensive that only the rich could afford them. A ritual so elaborate that only the initiated could follow it caused a division among the worshipers which gradually hardened into the caste system of modern India. A philosophy was developed which swept through the four stages of Materialism, Skepticism, Idealism, and Mysticism;[1] and a theology arose by the banks of the Ganges so profound in its speculations, so lofty in its aspiration, and widespread in its search for truth, that the logical mind of the West, used to the definitions which have their basis in historical facts and experiences, loses itself in the effort to thread the dimly lighted labyrinth of Oriental speculation. Unchecked by contact with other nations, and separated from the active life of the West, Brahmanism shows, in philosophy, in ritual, and in theology,

[1] Cousin's *History of Modern Philosophy*, vol. ii. Lecture V.

crudities and absurdities innumerable; so that it would be equally true to speak of Brahmanism as a splendid effort of the human mind to solve the problems of life, or to declare that it is a mass of ridiculous nonsense unworthy of the consideration of thoughtful men. And it would be quite possible, moreover, to draw from the recognized authorities of the Brahmanic religion passages which would bear out either assertion; but those who believe that God has not left himself without witness, in any nation, will seek for the good while not ignoring the evil; and will value the good all the more, knowing how easy it is for the human mind, even in its search after the highest truth, to be drawn aside by that which is unworthy of it. They will never cease to wonder that out of the corruptions of Hindu society there should have come thoughts which we may reverently compare with the words of our own Bible, and believe that they had the same source. The search for such traces of the influence of the Divine Spirit upon the lives of men will never lose its interest for the student of religion, — unless, indeed, he has somehow come to believe that the Revelation to Israel exhausted the divine reason, and that the Word did not lighten every man that has come into the world.

But before doing that, it may be well to try and fix in our minds certain landmarks by which our course may be guided; for Indian history is like the course of the river Ganges, which, continually overflowing its banks, leaves that which was the bed of last year miles away from the course which it follows now, so that it becomes more or less necessary to use the terms Vedic and Brahmanic in an arbitrary sense; for, while the historian may speak of the Vedic period as that time in which the events of the Maha-Bharata were being enacted, the student of the religious thought of India must confine it within stricter limits, and speak of the Vedic period as that age in which the hymns of the Rig-Veda were sung; which was an indefinite time before the year 1000 B. C. The next two hundred years lie on the border of both periods, and may be claimed by either.

It was during this time that the first code of laws was compiled, and ascribed to Manu, — that mysterious person whose name, like the Semitic Adam, is the generic name of the race, the ancestor of all living. The next great literary work of this period was the collection, and, to use a modern term, the editing, of the Rig-Veda. All this was done in the land of the five rivers before the people had taken those momentous steps which they could never retrace. Attention has already been called to the fact that in the Vedic period the father of the household was at once priest and king, but, when the age of conquest began, it was inevitable that there should come a differentiation of society, and that the work which originally had been done by one should become so difficult that it would require special training and a life devoted to its accomplishment.

The first work which presented itself to a people passing from the nomadic to the settled life was war. The warrior now lifts his head as a man distinct from the rest of the community. Of course the claims which would be put forth by such a class would not go unchallenged, and naturally also the challenge would be made in the name of what heretofore had been deemed supreme — religion. The conflict which now arose between the warrior and the priest is the same as meets us on every page of the history of mediæval Europe, and it ended in India, as in Europe, in a sort of compromise. That is to say, the priest, as the representative of religion, was theoretically admitted to be the superior of the warrior, but it was also insisted upon that the warrior should have the help of the supernatural power, at the disposal of the priest, in return for the protection of the secular arm. It was thus the caste system of India began. The priestly caste was called the Brahmin, and the warrior was called the Kshatriyas; and the laws of Manu declare the " sacerdotal order cannot prosper without the military, nor the military without the sacerdotal; and the prosperity of both, in this world and in the next, "depends on their cordial union."[1] Two classes having been evolved by the necessities of life, the rest of mankind naturally remained to form the other.

The Veisyas were the traders or the husbandmen, in a word, all who were neither priests nor soldiers. To this class there was added later a fourth, who were the aborigines of the conquered territory on which the great host was at this time moving. The Sudras, not belonging to the Aryan family, were counted beneath the consideration of the lowest of the conquering race.

[1] Elphinstone's *History of India*, vol. i.

So far there is nothing but what we would expect, indeed, nothing that we are not familiar with in the history of western Europe. It seems to be but one more illustration of the change of a community from "an indefinite homogeneity to a definite heterogeneity by the increase of the heterogeneity in the environment," and yet the term "Indian caste" has come to be the synonym of all that is hateful in the organization of society.

The answer that is sometimes given, that the evil in India was due to the impossibility of breaking the "cake of custom" has been shown to be unsatisfactory, but Mr. Fiske's attempt to account for that inability seems to be equally so. It will not do to say "the Oriental stage . . . is not a stage through which progressive nations pass, but it is a stage in which further progress is impossible, save through the occurrence of some deep-reaching social revolution."[1] India saw a social revolution which one would have supposed would have broken the "cake of custom," when Gautama began his work; and, indeed, it was broken, but there was no power in the revolution of Buddha to prevent its recementing. I believe the misery of caste has its origin in that thought of mankind which underlies the word itself. The Spanish word *casta*, from which caste is derived, means "a breed." The reason that it was so hard to break up this custom was, that it was associated with the deepest religious convictions of the Aryan people.

We have already seen that the fundamental belief

[1] *Outlines of Cosmic Philosophy*, vol. ii. By John Fiske.

in the universality of the divine, unenlightened by the revelation of the character of the divine, led to the association of the divine with that which somehow the human mind felt was unworthy of it; the consequence was that it became necessary to make formal distinctions, not only between things, but also between occupations, and then between men; until a belief arose in different " breeds " of men. Rome was saved from the caste system by belief in force, which was common to all men, but India could not accept such materialism as that. Greece was saved from it by faith in intelligence, but India could find no rest in rationalism. Judæa came very near to caste in Phariseeism, but there were other elements which counteracted that. Christianity brought into the world the belief in character, and faith in character is what lies back of democracy; the very antipode of caste. It was this failure to recognize character as the highest manifestation of the Divine life which first created caste, and afterwards made it well-nigh impossible to overcome the belief. It will never be overcome, save by the preaching of a gospel that " God has made of one all the children of men," and that to the highest possibility of humanity each man is called.

This belief in the necessity of arbitrary distinctions between things holy and unholy, having once taken possession of men's minds, was not likely to cease with the division of men into castes; it would permeate all society. The consequence was that it soon became impossible for any save those specially instructed in the mysteries, to perform them, and thus the priests became a necessity to all classes of men. That this followed as a natural consequence of the theories of life, of which we have already spoken, seems so plain that the popular explanation that the elaborate ritual was an invention of the priests, in order that they might fasten their hold upon the people, is no longer necessary. An artificial ritual was sure to follow the artificial distinctions among men and things, and then the necessity of a hierarchy would be apparent to all.

It was about this time that the Purohita (literally *præpositus*) or family chaplain to the great chiefs and nobles arose.[1] The next step was the division of the Brahmans themselves into different orders and the continuation of the Veda. The highest order of Brahmans was called "Hotri," and they alone were allowed to preside at the sacrifices, which had once been the privilege of every father of a family. But to the Rig-Veda was now added the Yagur-Veda, which consisted of a rich or hymn, and a dogmatic commentary on the same. Yagur-Veda, in which were embodied all the formulas for the sacrifices, was the special study of the second order or Adhvaryus. Last in order was the Sama-Veda the service book of the Udgatri or lowest order, whose business it was to chant the hymns at the sacrifice, which was actually performed by the Adhvaryus and presided over by the Hotri.

This process of adding to the sacred Canon, having begun, was continued later by the addition to

[1] *Satapatha Bráhmana.* Part I., by Julius Eggeling.

the Vedas of the Brahmanas, or authoritative commentaries of the Brahmans on the order of sacrifice. By this time the religion had traveled far from the life of the common people, and had become the very opposite of all that was worthy in the worship of the early Aryan herdsmen in the Punjab. The human conscience, which cannot ignore the existence of sin, which does not dare to ascribe sin to the Divine,[1] made the early Pantheism of their fathers impossible for men who had begun to recognize that there was such a thing as evil in the world. Faith in a divine person would have led to the revelation of righteousness, and in the absence of that faith it was inevitable that Brahmanism should sink to the degradation which it reached in the Athavangiras, or incantations, without which the sacrifice could not be propitious. Even should there be one failure at the end of a two days' ceremony the work must begin again.

While it is not necessary to account for the rise of the ceremonial by the supposition of the craft of the priests, no one can doubt what would follow on the belief that the formula of sacrifice was known to the priest alone, and that even for them, it was no easy matter to follow the intricacies of the ceremonial. The dignity of the priest was enhanced without an effort on his part, and the people became the prey of every evil-minded man who had been born a Brahman.

[1] Later the fatalism of India did lead, in the philosophy which preceded Buddhism, to this blasphemy, and that having been uttered, the caste system disappeared, until its revival in Hinduism. I believe that the assertion of caste was an attempt to escape the inevitable immorality of Pantheism.

And yet the Brahmanas are not altogether devoid of religious significance. The sacrifices may be divided into four classes: First those which were performed for a father in behalf of a son too young to perform them in his own person, concerning which there is nothing special to remark except the belief which underlay such an act, that in some way the young life was in relation with the divine life before it became conscious of the fact. The second great sacrifice was when the child came to maturity, and was invested with the sacred cord, when the son was said to be "born again." However limited may have been the idea connected with re-birth, the fact that such a thought should have been in the minds of the people, that the son of a Brahman was not necessarily pure, but needed by some voluntary act to assume the responsibility of a holy life, carries with it the promise of better things. Of the sacrifices on the lighting of the fire in the new home, and the sacrifices of the new moon and the full moon, it is not necessary to speak.

The Brahmanas, as we have already seen, contain not only the directions for the sacrifices, but a running commentary on the ceremony. And while in many cases, we may say in most, the reasons assigned for a particular act are puerile in the extreme, yet it is something that it should be thought desirable to give a reason for any act. A religion cannot be altogether debased that tries to give an account to its own reason of the things which it teaches as essential to salvation; and a very suggestive thing in the Brahmanas is that, not only do they pretend to give a reason for the performance of a particular act, but in nearly every case it is because in some way the gods have done the thing that is commanded. So that the man who lived under that system was constantly being stimulated by the remembrance that he was imitating the divine life, even though it were no more than in the pouring of ghee from one vessel into another. It was not a high religious life, but it had within it the germs of something better.

But it is not to the so-called religious books that we must look at this time to find the truest marks of the religious spirit that was striving to manifest itself amid the foolishness of Brahmanism. It has been well said that the code of Manu lays down "sound, solid, and practical morality." "The very ancient and always ingenious and suggestive symbolism which invests the majority of these usages is often of great beauty; and from the whole there stands forth the image of a life at once grave and lovable, and which, though bristling somewhat with formalities, is nevertheless serviceably active, and in nowise morose or inimicable to joyfulness of heart."[1]

And this code, it must be remembered, is not the production of one man, but is the embodiment of the real moral convictions of the people released somewhat, at least in this department of life, from the trammels of the religious ceremonial.

It cannot be too often repeated that all these sacrifices were not intended to propitiate the gods. They may have been so thought of at times, but in

[1] *The Religions of India.* By A. Barth, trans. by J. Wood, p. 53.

the teachings of the Brahmans there was no thought of expiation. The simple Vedic belief in the participation of the gods in the family meal led, as we have already seen, to a belief that the gods were in some way nourished by the sacrifices, and that in turn gave way to a belief in the entire dependence of the gods upon the right performance of the ceremonies. In this way all spirituality passed from the rites, and they became a mechanical performance in which the worshiper was, as it were, one of the cogs in the wheel that must ever keep moving or else destruction would fall upon gods and men alike. To the sacrifices then was given the name *Karman*, a word destined to play a most important part in the religious history of India. No one, gods or men, is free from the necessity of sacrifice, or rather not from sacrifice, for that implies a spiritual act, but from the mechanical act of the ceremonial. Brahmanism reached no lower depth than this, and yet I believe that it was indeed the shadow cast by a great truth which their minds were no longer able to receive, and of which we must speak again, after we have considered the attempt which was made by philosophy to lift Brahmanism from its degradation.

This philosophy is embodied in the Upanishads. The word comes from a root which means to "sit down," and from that original idea of sitting at the feet of a teacher it came to mean "submission," and finally, because of what was taught, the word came to mean revelation. The Upanishads belong to that division of the Brahmanas called the Aranyakas, or forest readings. The word is suggestive; it shows that a time had come when men could no longer rest satisfied with the performance of a ceremonial; they found it necessary to meditate, and endeavor in some way to renew that intercourse with the divine life which had been the glory of the Vedic period. They withdrew then to the forests; they abandoned the ceremonial, and tried by meditation and fasting to draw near to God. Around these hermits disciples began to gather, and the great problems of life, which the performance of no rite can ever solve, were brought to these holy men, and the answers written down by those who felt that wisdom was the best heritage for their children. It was not long before the value of the Upanishads was recognized, and when the Brahmanas were admitted as a part of the Vedas it was said that the very essence and glory of the Vedas was the Upanishads.

The three words which give us the key to the Upanishads are Sât, Âtman and Brâhma. We have seen that in the last development of Vedic thought the Rishis had come to speak of the divine essence as a neuter principle of life manifesting itself in a glorious body in the manifold phenomena of nature; but when, by the advance of civilization, men had been drawn from that close contact with nature which was a part of the daily life of the authors of the Vedic hymns, and society had come to take that form in the village life which it has never lost to this day; when schools were opened, and temples built, and bazaars sprang up in the crowded streets;

the field, so to speak, for the divine manifestation, had changed from nature to man. So the religious teachers began now to speak less and less of Asura and more and more of Sât.

By Sât they meant what we mean by reality, what the Greeks called Τὸ ὄν. What is the unchangeable reality? What is the real thing that lies back of all phenomena in nature and in man? That was the question. They never doubted that there was a reality; the problem was how to come near to it. What relation did it bear to nature? What relation did it bear to all apparent forms of life? The things which we speak of as real they said were unreal; that everything which was seen was an illusion, but that back of all illusion lay the self-existent unseen reality. The authors of the Upanishads would have claimed as their own the words of the Christian poet: —

> Change and decay in all around I see;
> O Thou who changest not, abide with me!

The *Karman* of which the Brahmans had spoken, the endless chain which bound gods and men alike to the ceremonial, these teachers of the Upanishads recognized to be far more than a ceremonial law. Cause worked itself out in effect; the effect itself became a cause. All life was an endless chain of birth and re-birth, but at the centre of all the eddies of life there was eternal calm, — there was Sât.

But the cause of the rise of philosophy was not an interest in speculation; far from it. Philosophy was but a means to an end, which was escape from the burden of existence. That any one should deliberately devote himself to any other end is, to the Hindu, incomprehensible.

Any one who has been in India, and has come in contact with the high caste natives, must have been struck with the silent contempt with which they view the English triumphs in engineering. Road building and all other evidences of material progress are to them what the lifting of a heavy stone would be to a scholar of feeble frame. They do not envy the men who can do these things; they only wonder that they should care to do them! The Hindu mind has changed but little in two thousand years, and the problem then as now has always been how to escape from the illusion of life and find peace in Yoga, that is, in union with the unchangeable reality. Of course, it was not possible to prevent questions arising in the minds of their scholars in regard to the great mysteries of life, but all the efforts of the teacher were directed to diverting them from any thought which did not tend directly to Yoga. Thus, in the beginning of the Svetasvatara Upanishad,[1] we read, "The Brahma students say: Is Brahman the cause? Whence are we born? Whereby do we live, and whither do we go? O ye who know Brahman, tell us at whose command we abide, whether in pain or in pleasure?" But the teachers would turn them from all speculation, and so bade them meditate on Brahman as he is revealed in the heart of man; in that way only can they

---

[1] In quoting from the Upanishads the translation of *The Sacred Books of the East*, ed. by F. Max Müller is used, and the references will be made to them.

hope to attain to the knowledge of the sages who know God as he is in himself, which, when a man knows, "all fetters fall off," sufferings are destroyed, and birth and death cease.[1]

In that state a man realizes the Yoga, that is, the union of the divine within and without. Before that union could be effected, however, it was necessary that the distinctions in the divine should be recognized.

The reality which lay at the root of all the illusions of life they called, as we have seen, Sât. Yet that word seldom, if ever, occurs in the Upanishads. The reason is, that the authors of the later Vedas had two other words which they used to express the divine life: one was Brahman and the other was Âtman, and Sât was the reality in which these two manifestations of it existed; to use terms borrowed from Christian theology, Om is the Οὐσία of which Sât, Âtman, and Brahman are the Ὑποστάσεις.

It was Sât who later was named by the mysterious syllable Om. This word, which originally meant "That" or "Yea," expressed with sublime simplicity all that in the last resort they could say of the eternal life that it is the eternal yea.

Om means Brahman. Om means all this. Om means obedience.

Beyond the senses is the mind. Beyond the mind is the highest created Being. Higher than that Being is the Great Self. Higher than the Great is the highest Undeveloped. Beyond the Undeveloped is the Person, the all-pervading and entirely imperceptible. Every creature

[1] *Sacred Books of the East*, vol. xv. p. 231.

that knows him is liberated, and obtains immortality. His form is not to be seen. No one beholds him with the eye. He is imagined by the heart, by wisdom, by the mind. Those who know this are immortal.[1]

The person with a thousand heads, a thousand eyes, a thousand feet, having compassed the earth on every side extends beyond it by ten fingers' breadth.[2]

Its hands and feet are everywhere; its eyes and head are everywhere; its ears are everywhere; it stands encompassing all in the world.[3]

The face of the True is covered with a golden disk. Open that, O Sun, that we may see the nature of the True.

O Sun, only seer, . . . spread thy rays and gather them!

The light which is the fairest form, I see it. I am what he is. Breath to air and to the immortal! Then this my body ends in ashes. Om! Mind! remember! Remember thy deeds! Mind, remember! Remember thy deeds!

Agni lead us on to beatitude by a good path, thou O God who knowest all things! Keep far from us crooked evil, and we shall offer thee the fullest praise.[4]

Lord of the Universe glory to thee! Thou art the Self of all; thou art the maker of all, the enjoyer of all; thou art all life, and the lord of all pleasures and joy. Glory to thee, the tranquil, the deeply hidden, the incomprehensible, the immeasurable, without beginning and without end.[5]

But it was impossible that the religious want could be satisfied by a life so far removed from man; and

---

[1] *Sacred Books of the East*, vol. xv. p. 22.
[2] That is, beyond man's power of computation.
[3] *Sacred Books of the East*, vol. xv. p. 247.
[4] Ibid. vol. xv. p. 199.
[5] Ibid. vol. xv. p. 303.

so, while the unchangeable reality was often spoken of as Brahman or breath, still it is in terms that imply the distance that stretches between the human and the divine. So the problem that always perplexed them was, how the individual who in his nature is partaker of the illusions of life is to reach the Sât who is at the centre of all?

They answered that problem by asserting that in every individual there is also dwelling the eternal reality which when so considered they called Âtman. This word Âtman is translated in the "Sacred Books of the East" by the English word "self." But we shall make a great mistake if we suppose that by the word "self" they meant the individual life. "To enter one's self" meant "to know the Âtman;" but when they spoke of "self" they meant that eternal reality which existed not only at the centre of all life but also dwelt in the individual.

As we read the Upanishads we find that they sometimes use the word Brahman as synonymous with Âtman: thus they will say, "One must know the Âtman," or, "one must know the Brahman." They were convinced that if they could know the Âtman or the Brahman, they could reach that calm which all the disturbances and eddies of life circle round but never move.

No wonder they longed for release when this is what they thought of life.

O Saint, what is the use of the enjoyment of pleasures in this offensive, pithless, body — a mere mass of bones, sinews, skin, marrow, flesh, seed, blood, mucus, tears, phlegm, ordure, water, bile, and slime! What is the use of the enjoyment of pleasures in the body which is assailed by lust, hatred, greed, delusion, fear, anguish, jealousy, separation from what is loved, union with what is not loved, hunger, thirst, old age, illness, grief, and other evils?[1]

Now the way of escape from all these miseries was by "knowledge." But here let us guard against a misunderstanding of terms. The Hindu mind had no interest in the search for truth, as such. The playful skepticism of the Greek mind, which played at battledoor and shuttlecock with the problems of life, the Hindu would have regarded with unspeakable disgust. The playful agnosticism of Socrates would have seemed to them impious. They were much more in accord with the utilitarianism of modern physical science, though words would have failed them to express their contempt for men who deliberately devoted themselves to the utilization of material things while the reality, which alone could deliver from endless miseries, was still undiscovered: such an one was like a man who should carve out figures from the morning mist and dream that they would remain as monuments of his genius! "The only subject," says Prof. Monier Williams,[2] "which has power to rouse them from their normal condition of mental torpor is religion." Philosophy then was to them only a means to an end, and every statement of philosophy must be interpreted by its religious bearing: so when they say that peace is to be ob-

[1] *Sacred Books of the East*, vol. xv. p. 288.
[2] *Religious Thought and Life in India*.

tained by "knowledge" we must understand that the authors of the Upanishads were in the habit of speaking of the religious ceremonies as "ignorance," so that "knowledge" originally meant meditation as opposed to ritual. But their minds could not rest satisfied with a mere negation, and so we find them speaking of "knowledge" as the acquaintance with the esoteric teaching of the Vedas as opposed to a familiarity with the routine of the sacrifices.

Indeed to him who thus knows this Brahma-Upanishad (*i. e.*, the secret doctrine of the Vedas) the sun does not rise and set. For him there is day once and for all. A father may tell that doctrine of Brahma to his eldest son, or to a worthy pupil. But no one should tell it to any one else, even if he gave him the whole sea-girt earth, full of treasures; for this doctrine is worth more than that, yea it is worth more.[1]

But there was a farther step yet taken in this definition of knowledge. It was not enough to identify it with acquaintance with certain formulas of the Veda to which perhaps a purely arbitrary interpretation might be given; and so we find in the Upanishads "knowledge" spoken of as the New Testament speaks of "faith," as the exercise of the spiritual nature so as to identify one's self with the object of faith or knowledge. In the second Kanda of the Mundaka Upanishad we read, "He who knows the Self, knows that highest home of Brahman, in which all is contained and shines brightly. The wise who, without desiring happiness, worships

[1] *Sacred Books of the East*, vol. i. p. 44.

that person, transcends his seed," *i. e.*, he is not born again.[1]

That Self cannot be gained by the Veda, nor by understanding, nor by much learning. He whom the Self chooses, by him the Self can be gained, when the Self chooses him (his body) as his own.

Nor is that Self to be gained by one who is destitute of strength, or without earnestness, or without right meditation. But if the wise man strives after it by these means . . . then his Self enters into the home of Brahman.

When they have reached him (the Self) the sages become satisfied through knowledge, they are conscious of their Self, their passions have passed away, and they are tranquil. The wise, having reached him who is omnipresent everywhere,[2] devoted to the Self, enter into him wholly.

As the flowing rivers disappear in the sea, losing their name and their form, thus a wise man, freed from name and form, goes to the divine person, who is greater than the great (*i. e.*, than self).

He who knows that highest Brahman becomes even Brahman. In his race no one is born ignorant of Brahman. He overcomes evil; free from the fetters of the heart, he becomes immortal.[3]

---

[1] *Sacred Books of the East*, vol. xv. p. 40.

[2] This is not a mere tautology. Brahmanic Pantheism was the belief that God was *equally* present everywhere. The consequence was that it was unable to emphasize the quality of the divine presence. That necessitates the predication of personality. While it is true to say that God is omnipresent, meaning (as Coleridge says) that "all things are present to God," it is equally true to say that in Jesus, as in no one else, "dwelt all the fulness of the Godhead bodily." That was a distinction Brahmanism could not make, for it never predicated "quality" of God.

[3] *Sacred Books of the East*, vol. xv. pp. 40, 41.

Knowledge then meant self-knowledge. To know that in one's self dwelt the Eternal; that in it man had his being would bring peace, would assure man that he was not a creature of a moment, would lead him to feel that his home was with the Eternal. So Sât, Om, Brahman, was called Âtman, Self.

See how wonderfully this is expressed in the Khandogya-Upanishad.

The intelligent, whose body is spirit, whose form is light, whose thoughts are true, whose nature is like ether (omnipresent and invisible), from whom all works, all desires, all sweet odors and tastes proceed; he who embraces all this, who never speaks and is never surprised, he is myself within the heart, smaller than a corn of barley, smaller than a mustard seed. . . . He also is myself within the heart, greater than the earth, greater than the sky, greater than heaven, greater than all these worlds.

He from whom all works, all desires, all sweet odors and tastes proceed, who embraces all this, who never speaks and is never surprised, he is myself within the heart, is that Brahman. When I shall have departed hence I shall obtain that Âtman.[1]

Let me quote one more saying before leaving this wonderful history of man's thought of God.

Know that the person within all beings, not heard here, not reached, not thought, not subdued, not seen, not understood, not classed, but hearing, thinking, seeing, classing, sounding, understanding, knowing, is the Self.[2]

This Sât Brahma, Âtman is Om, is One.[3]

[1] *Sacred Books of the East*, vol. i. p. 48.
[2] Ibid.
[3] Prof. Williams would make Brahma — from a root meaning

He who dwells in the water and within the water, whom the water does not know, whose body the water is, and who rules the water within, he is thyself, the ruler within, the immortal.[1]

For the man who has by knowledge identified himself with the Eternal there remains the immortal life, the life freed from all the miseries because delivered from the illusion.

By the old age of the body that does not age; by the death of the body that is not killed.[2]

The Brahman is the true being set in the body. It is the Self; free from sin, free from old age, free from death and grief, from hunger and thirst; which desires and imagines nothing but what it has.

For those who know this, death is but the casting away of a dead body, as the snake sloughs off its skin on an ant-hill, that the immortal Self may enter into the unconditioned Self.

But on the other hand —

Those who depart from hence without having discovered the Self and those true desires, for them there is no freedom in all the worlds.[3]

The true desires are hidden by what is false, as people who do not know the country walk again and again over the gold treasure that has been hidden somewhere in the earth and do not discover it. Thus do all those creatures

"to increase" — the "Essence," and Sât and Âtman manifestations thereof, but the theological thought of the Upanishads seems to have been in a state of flux, so that almost anything may find support.

[1] *Sacred Books of the East*, vol. xv. p. 133.
[2] Ibid. vol. i. p. 126.
[3] Ibid. vol. i. p. 127.

do who going into the Brahma-world yet do not discover it, because they are carried away by untruth. They do not discover the true Self in Brahman, that Self which abides in the heart.[1]

It is easy to see how such a doctrine might be corrupted; and we have the story of a great misunderstanding on the part of certain of the disciples. We are told that on one occasion certain men came to a learned teacher and besought him to instruct them in the way of Self, and he replied, "The person that is seen in the eye, that is the Self;"[2] by which he meant, the image that is beheld with the inward eye and not with the eye of sense. But they supposing him to mean the minute image which every child has seen and wondered at, asked if they beheld this image reflected in a mirror or in the water would that be seeing the "Self," to which the sage contemptuously replies "yes." So they go their way and adorn themselves in their best clothes, and then looking into the water, and beholding the image of themselves reflected therein, return and say that they have seen the "Self;" and as they depart the sage says in bitter irony, " they both go away without having perceived and without having known the Self, and whosoever will follow this doctrine will perish. But they went their way and preached that men should worship the self, *i. e.*, the body, and that whosoever will worship the self and serve the self will gain both this world and the next!"[3]

[1] *Sacred Books of the East*, vol. i. p. 129.
[2] Ibid. vol. i. p. 135.
[3] Ibid vol. i. pp. 133–135.

These extracts will be enough to bring before our minds clearly the fundamental doctrines of Brahmanism; it remains now to compare them with the Gospel of the Christ. But this cannot be done as the Master himself would have done it, unless we approach the subject with reverence. Nothing is more truly atheistic than the tone in which men sometimes speak of the solemn speech of God's children concerning what he has done for their souls. Let us avoid that error and recognize that while it was incomplete, growing up in the midst of human corruption and sin, while there is much that is false, much that is absurd, much that was unworthy of men to whom the Spirit of God was speaking, yet in the sacred book of Brahmanism there is essential truth. First, then, we find a statement of the truth that spiritual things can only be spiritually discerned, and that the glory of man's life consisteth not in the abundance of the things which he possesses, but in his recognition of the indwelling of the divine life. And if this be so, whence came it? To say that it was man's discovery while truths which were developed through the history of Israel were God's revelation, is to strike at the root of all religion: for it is to assert that what is true may come apart from God! It denies that God "has made of one" all nations, "that they might seek after him and find him." "Every good gift and every perfect gift is from above, and cometh down from the Father of Lights in whom is no variableness, neither shadow of turning." The truth in Israel was God's revelation to Israel, the truth in India was God's revelation to the Hindu. But this spiritual sympathy with what they received must not blind our eyes to their failure to make the most of the truth committed to them, and the results of that failure are not difficult to find.

The first downward step was taken, as we have seen, when they caused the natural distinctions in society to harden into the caste system, — a system so rigid that no change has been able permanently to overthrow it. This belief in caste made any real gospel to the poor impossible — even made it seem undesirable. So that all the sublime spiritual truths which we acknowledge with delight were for a very limited class of society. It is true that the best minds could not rest satisfied with the caste system as it first took shape. We have seen that the sacrifices preached the necessity of a new birth even for the Brahman, and later it was said that no man could attain to Self whom the Self did not choose. Had they been able to follow out the path that the thought of election opened before them the result might have been different; it might have led them to ask themselves the purpose that lay back of election; they might have laid hold of the sublime teaching of Israel, that election is the witness to the divine care for all, and thus the caste system might have been broken. But it was not so. They asserted that the Self chose only those who were strong and serious and self-denying; but that doctrine only served to intensify their belief in individual merit, and so lay the whole burden of salvation upon the individual. The consequence was that, having first separated the

Brahman class from all others, and then separated the Brahmans themselves into the elect and the non-elect, and having insisted that this election was the result of individual merit, they developed a self-consciousness which became unbearable, and salvation presented itself to them as escape from this individuality which was a burden too heavy for them to bear.

If we turn now from the early Brahmanic theory of man to the belief in the divine life, we shall see that they came nearer to the truth. We have seen that the sacrifices were enjoined as imitations of certain godlike deeds. The authors of the Brahmanas even asserted that the creation of the world was an act accompanied by sacrifices. Now leaving out of sight the gross form which this thought assumed,— the cutting up of a huge giant — is there not really a profound truth hidden in this teaching? I think so. They could not but feel that in some way the divine life must participate in that which was such an essential part of human life. The grossest form of heathen sacrifice has witnessed to man's belief that there was something magnanimous in the divine nature, for I do not believe any people have believed that they could make a payment which would satisfy the divine demand; they must always have felt that they would show their good intention, and trust that the will would be accepted for the deed. And if this was true of those sacrifices which were ostensibly propitiatory in their nature, much more must it have been so of those of which we are now speaking. In some way the Hindus felt that the divine life had experienced sacrifice.

Now that is a belief into which the teaching of Christ fits exactly. The cross of Jesus is not the revelation of an awful violation of the divine nature; it is the revelation of the divine life. Sacrifice becomes painful, " exceeding sorrowful, even unto death," only because it is done in an atmosphere of sin. The sacrifice of Jesus was the witness to the essential divinity of sacrifice. " I have power to lay down my life, and I have power to take it again; this commandment have I received of my father." " Therefore my Father loveth me, because I lay down my life that I might take it again." The divine life then, whether it is considered as Father or Son, delights in sacrifice. It was with that truth in mind that St. Peter wrote of Jesus, " He was the lamb slain before the foundation of the world." We can claim then as divine truth the Brahmanic belief that creation was an act of sacrifice.

Yet when we try to bring these two thoughts together, we see the weakness of the whole Brahmanic system. There seems to have been no power in the Hindu mind to compare " spiritual things with spiritual." If a Brahman found a pearl of great price, he would not sell all that he had and buy it! He would simply be content to gaze at it.

It would never occur to him that it might be utilized, he would never expect to find another, and if he did he would have no power to join the two. He would simply meditate upon its beauty in the hope that by such meditation he might grow like it, and in that way " shuffle off " this " too, too solid flesh." That is why Brahmanism failed in its attempts to attain Yoga, or union with the divine, and so yielded to the efforts of Buddha. It was by the recognition of sacrifice as the essence of the divine life, and participation in that sacrifice, that Jesus said escape from the bondage of this world lay. "If any man will do God's will he shall know of the doctrine," and that truth (or doctrine) he said would make men free. But it seems never to have occurred to the Brahmanic mind so to utilize truth! They said that what they longed for was union with the divine life. But when we look at the character of that union we see that it was not the Christian atonement, but what they called "aloneness." That is to say, what they wanted was that the Self which dwelt in their body should so absorb their individuality that nothing but that Self would remain. That they thought would bring them peace. But humanity cannot so easily destroy itself as that. No real peace, the history of the human soul has shown, can come, save through the consciousness of the atonement. "I and my Father are one." Yet "My Father is greater than I." "Glorify me, O Father, with the glory which I had with thee before the worlds were." It is eternal life to know the Father and the Son. The consciousness of union can only follow the consciousness of distinction. A distinction which is the result of the mysterious act of "begetting." With profound spiritual insight, the creed asserts that the eternal Son is begotten, not made. He is an impartation of the divine life. The faith of the Church is that but one has realized that Sonship, but that all are created to realize it. The Upanishads said, " Sacrifice because the Devas sacrificed, but the one thing needful is knowledge, for that will result in "aloneness." The gospel says the one thing needful is faith; faith is sacrificial in its character and therefore divine. Perfect faith is perfect atonement, and perfect atonement is knowledge of Father and Son.

The more we look into this wonderful system the more profoundly are we impressed with its anticipation of Christian truth, and yet at its failure to appreciate the bearing of that truth. We have seen one illustration of this: look now at that fundamental Brahmanic belief that the one reality, Sât alone, remains " the same yesterday, to-day, and forever." The words of St. John are truly Brahmanic: " All that is in the world, the lust of the flesh, and the lust of the eyes, and the pride of life, are not of the Father but are of the world, and the world passeth away, and the lust thereof." But when he added, " He that doeth the will of God abideth forever," it would have meant nothing to them, because they knew of no *will* in the sense in which that word is used in the Bible, — the self-conscious participation in the divine purpose.

For Sât had no purpose. Purpose implies good or evil intent — they would not have ascribed evil purpose, but they could not have ascribed good — the essence of the reality was unmoved and unmovable indifference. Sât was nothing but power. It is here that the divergence between the gospel of Jesus and Brahmanism is the greatest. Jesus's teaching is full of the thought of the power of God, but it is always spoken of as a power mighty to save. The power of God is the power of a father; it is simply thought of as love manifesting itself against selfishness; we are conscious of power only because we see that there is friction.

The Brahman sits dumb before the immensity of divine power; Jesus thinks of the divine power as the possibility that lies in the background, and says: "Father, all things are possible with thee, do not let my will be done!" The God of Jesus is a God who is love.

In the doctrine of Âtman again we see the same approximation and subsequent recoil. The real life of the divine is in the heart of man. "Do not think of the divine life as far off;" the Upanishads are saying on every page, "it is near; it is in the heart of man."[1] But Jesus said the same, "The kingdom of God is within you." "Realize the true Self," said Brahmanism; in the parable of the Prodigal Son Jesus set his seal to the truth of this teaching, when he declared that when the wanderer turned from the illusions of life "He came to him*self*." You cannot know what the "Highest Uncreated Being is unless you see Him in the life of man." That is the very essence of the gospel. "No man hath seen God at any time; the only begotten which is in the bosom of the Father, He hath declared Him."

But here again the parallel ceases. The result

---

[1] A favorite saying was: "The City of Brahman is the body of man." Like St. Paul's saying: "Your body is the temple of the Holy Ghost."

of Âtmanship is the destruction of humanity. The result of Sonship is the glorification of humanity. " Father, I will that they whom thou hast given me be with me where I am, that they may behold my glory." The whole gospel abounds with the joy of redemption, the atonement with God. It is the long story of the "riches of the glory of his inheritance in the saints."

The same characteristics meet us in the next article of the Brahmanic creed. For in the word *Brahman* they seem again to have anticipated the gospel. For Brahman means breath. And they believed that man could breathe that breath into himself and so participate in the divine life. But when we come to look into the matter a little more closely, we find that the word means to them nothing but breath. There seems to be no such subtle distinction as we find in the gospel between the "blowing wind and the breathing Spirit." In other words, Brahman was without character. The consequence was that Brahmanism was without hope. There was never the divine intoxication of joy such as we read of in the gospel as following the consciousness of the Spirit's indwelling, so marked that it led the unbelievers to ascribe the joyful outburst to the " drunkenness of new wine." There came with the inbreathing of Brahman no sense of a comforter, a teacher, leading into truth. It may be said that such effects could only follow the revelation of the divinity of humanity by the incarnation; but Brahmanism had no prophecy of such a dispensation as we find in the Hebrew prophets.

And the reason of this is to be found, I think, in the fact that they were utterly ignorant of the Hebrew experience of "the pouring out of the Spirit," all that they knew of was the *in*breathing of the divine breath, and the result was not spiritual intoxication; it was loss of spiritual consciousness. They partook not of a stimulant, but of a drug!

Yet no man who knows that these men were striving to know the truth should doubt that the Father of All saw them, felt them feeling after Him if haply they might find Him. When we remember that this was their creed: the belief in the divine as the one reality; the belief that in every Brahman that reality dwelt; the belief that if man could once know that image he would see Him who is invisible; the belief that for that man must in some way breathe the divine life into himself; the belief that the result of this struggle against the illusion of life, though it be for the present painful, will, in the end, be the perfection of life, in which there will be no more sorrow, no more parting, no more pain; no man who knows that ought to hesitate to say of Brahmanism, "It was not far from the kingdom of God."

Yet it was not the kingdom of God, for this Sât, Brahman, and Âtman, wherever found, was essentially *inert*.[1] It was, as they constantly said, a "treasure hid in a field;" it had no power to bring itself to the surface; man must seek for it

---

[1] Since this was written, attention has been called to the same characteristic in the writings of Plato. "In the *Timæus*, he pictures God as the passive Deity, at an infinite distance in the

and find it. The consequence was that men divided themselves into two classes; those who sought for release from illusion by ceremonial rites, and those who reached out for Âtmanship by an act of the will. The Upanishads recognize both; the first they call the way of ignorance, which it is admitted must be the path for most men; but the more excellent way is a counsel of perfection, to which only a few are expected to attain. But the outcome of both was the same; those who practiced the ceremonial did not find the peace they sought, and consequently increased the intensity of their austerities until they degenerated into the fearful, revolting, and degrading self-inflicted tortures of modern India, which are supposed by many educated people to be the essence of Brahmanism.

On the other hand, there were the philosophers who sought for Sât by an act of the will, which, beginning with meditation, ended in a condition hardly to be distinguished from stupor. The end in both ways was the same, — the destruction of the active powers of mind or body.

It is just here that the doctrine of Jesus, so akin to Brahmanism, takes its place. No Brahman ever preached the doctrine of Sât more earnestly than Jesus. Almost his last words were, " To this end

---

heavens, unable to come into immediate contact with a world of which the very materials contain the conditions of evil." (*Continuity of Christian Thought*, by A. V. G. Allen, p. 43.) It is here suggested that this is akin to Buddhism, but I venture to think that it is rather akin to Brahmanism. God did not appear inert to Buddha because of the prevalence of evil, but because the only God of whom he had heard was the Brahmanic God who was *essentially* inert.

was I born, and for this cause came I into the world that I might bear witness unto the truth," unto the one reality, unto Sât.

It is the same with the doctrine of Âtman. When at the last the perplexed disciples ask, by the mouth of Philip, for a revelation of the invisible God which could not be doubtful, Jesus answered, "Have I been so long with you and hast thou not known me, Philip? He that hath seen me hath seen the Father also."

Now all this was Brahmanic doctrine, only no Brahman had ever been able to announce himself as the Âtman, and had he done so the instinct of humanity would have revolted against him, for in such a case there must be success or the most ignominious failure. Yet this is what Jesus dared; declared that he was the Âtman, the one perfect image of the invisible Sât, and yet claimed all men as sharers in that eternal Âtmanship, and could offer for them no higher prayer than that they might be conscious of that truth, "I in them and thou in me, that they may be made perfect in One."

Now had the gospel stopped here it would only have shown a remarkable coincidence between Semitic and Aryan speculation, but it went farther. If St. Paul had been acquainted with the Upanishads, he could not have rebuked the Brahmans more perfectly than he has done in the Epistle to the Romans, where, warning his people against the effort to find God, he says, "Say not in thy heart who shall ascend into heaven, or who shall descend into the deep," for the good news has been brought you that

God is *seeking you*, and, that you may be redeemed from the body of death, the Word is in your "mouth and in your heart."

The revelation of God as Sât, the revelation of Jesus — and so of humanity as the Âtman, would not be complete without the revelation of the divine life as an energizing spirit seeking for that which, amid the illusions of life, is lost. If we might epitomize the teaching of Brahmanism, we would say that it is to be found in the first part of the parable which tells us of the son who "came to him*self*," and began to seek his father; but the gospel of Jesus is all told in that same parable where the divine is pictured, not as waiting in supreme indifference for that return, but as a father who saw the son "a long way off and *ran* and fell on his neck and kissed him."

This is indeed the typical parable, but it is so because it embodies that which was, all through the gospel, the revelation of God's self-impartation. The eternal unchangeable reality condescends to man's weakness that it may reveal itself. The truth speaks so as to be understood by "babes and sucklings." The "image of the unseen God" is seen and handled of men. The shepherd seeks the sheep that is lost. The king dies that the subject may be drawn in loyalty to him.

In its analysis, if such a word may be used, of the divine being, Brahmanism was not far from the statements of Christian theology. In its faith that rest could only be found in union; it bore witness to the truth; but where it failed was in its ignorance of grace, the spirit "helping our infirmities," and so leading through a Saviour to a Father. That this is not a mere guess will be seen when we come to Brahmanism in its later form of Hinduism, where it will be found that "grace" was the thought which underlay the revival after the expulsion of the Buddhists.

CHAPTER IV.

THE TRANSITION FROM BRAHMANISM TO BUDDHISM.

We have spoken of Brahmanism as if it consisted of a uniform system of thought. But this is far from being the case. The fundamental ideas are the same indeed, in all the systems, but it was not long before Indian philosophy divided into two distinct lines, diverging more and more from a common principle. It forms no part of the plan of this book to enter into a consideration of Indian metaphysics, but it will be necessary to glance hurriedly at the pathway which philosophic speculation took in the seventh century before our era; for there we shall find at once the cause of the decline of Brahmanism and the rise of Buddhism.

It was, perhaps, the somewhat feeble rationalism of the Brahmanas, that caused the rise of the Mimansa school.

It can hardly be called a philosophy and is not so counted by writers on the history of philosophy; it was rather the expression of a reaction against the too free handling of religious questions. "The foundation of belief and conduct," said Djaimini, the founder of the Mimansa, "is to be discovered in the Vedas; to them we must turn."[1] If it was objected that the real difficulty consists in finding the meaning of the Vedas, the answer was ready. "It is to be found, not by speculation, but by tradition. What have the holy men of old declared they were taught by their fathers? That is the way to find the truth. Alongside of the letter there has come the tradition which interprets the letter. From the solution of speculative questions, which, as we have seen, never had special interest for the Hindu mind, the school of Mimansa went on to solve questions of conscience by the same infallible rule of '*Quod semper quod ubique quod ab omnibus.*'" The chief interest of the Mimansa school lies in the fact that it was the precursor of the Vedanta school, of which we shall speak in a moment.

At the opposite pole of thought is found the system of Gautama,[2] called the Nyaya or "Analysis." The word analysis is sufficient to assure us that this school would not be destined to have great influence in India. The Indian mind is impatient of delay in the discovery of the goal which it seeks; if that be at once pointed out, then the teacher may spend the rest of life in developing the results of the discovery, but the "Deliverance" must not be delayed. Therefore the Nyaya school with its hair-splitting distinctions, which promised so much and led to nothing, had no such career in India as it had in Greece, where the delight was not in the discovery but in the search for truth.

[1] Cousin, vol. ii. Lect. V.
[2] Not of course to be confounded with Sakyamouni.

TRANSITION FROM BRAHMANISM TO BUDDHISM. 95

Probably because of this inability to continue long in the analysis of thought, the Nyaya school passed into the Veiseshika, or philosophy of physical research. The outcome was the anatomical theory of the universe, ending in materialism, and, except in the stronger few, in the lowest form of Epicureanism. "So long as life lasts, delight thyself and live well; when once the body is reduced to ashes, it will revive no more." [1]

It was when Indian thought had reached the chaos that was sure to follow on the enunciation of Epicureanism that there arose a school of thought which declared that the solution of the problem of life was to be found only by determining to what the origin of life is to be ascribed. Kapila, the founder of the great Sankhyan philosophy, took up the problem of life where it had been dropped by the Veiseshikan school.

Kapila had no quarrel with that school because of its methods; he complained because it did not go far enough. It may be true that the origin of the visible universe is the result of the "fortuitous concourse of atoms," but to what are we to ascribe the origin of the atoms? It would be instructive — if our subject were the history of philosophy — to note how in ancient days, as now, all attempts to account for the things which are seen lead sooner or later to

---

[1] This anticipation of "let us eat and drink for to-morrow we die" is attributed to the Sokâyatas, an obscure sect, which analogy would lead us to conclude was an offshoot of the Veiseshikan. See *Religions of India*, Barth, p. 86.

the introduction of a principle which is not seen. The unknown and unknowable mystery back of all phenomena of Herbert Spencer has been antedated by the Prakriti of Kapila. Prakriti seems to have been an ethereal principle of life having the power of self-fertilization. What is needed, said Kapila, is knowledge of the universe, and that will save men from all the miseries of illusion. And that knowledge is to be obtained neither by meditation, nor by the analysis of the mind, nor by the voice of tradition, but by sensation. Matter produces sensation and sensation produces intelligence. Where there is no sensation there is no intelligence. In other words, we can know nothing which cannot be apprehended by the senses.[1] Of course all this did not pass without protest. The idea of cause and effect, it was answered, does not come from sensation: whence comes it? The idea of cause and effect, answered Kapila, is a delusion; it has no sensible basis. Cause is only a preceding effect. If nature had never existed it could never have been created, for there would have been nothing with which to create it. Nature is its own cause. Nature is the cause of intelligence. There can, therefore, be no intelligence higher than nature; there can be no God.

The great rival of the Sankhyan philosophy was the Vedantan which, as we have seen, was an outgrowth of the Mimansa. The school of authority was compelled to let in the reason as an arbiter

[1] A full account of this system will be found in Cousin, vol. ii. Lect. V.

along with tradition and so while the Vedantan school, as its name implies,[1] pretended to reverence authority, it soon became in the best sense rationalistic. Its history is not unlike that of English Protestantism, which attempted to have two standards of faith, the tradition of the fathers and the conscience. And perhaps for the same reason — that it seemed to answer the two different needs that men have always experienced, not only of having a truth commend itself to their individual conscience, but also of knowing that the individual conscience is in harmony with the universal thought of humanity as far as that can be ascertained — the Vedantan philosophy became the great bulwark to stem the rising tide of skepticism.

Like every other Indian philosophy it began with the problem of escape. "Who will deliver me from the body of this death," was as truly the cry of the perplexed Hindu as of the sin-smitten Hebrew. But to escape, the Pundits of the Vedanta school recognized that they must follow the lead of Kapila and define the "Illusion." As "*ex nihilo nihil fit*" was an axiom from which all Indian speculation began, they had to make choice of one of the horns of the dilemma. That it was possible to begin by premising that matter is an expression of mind never occurred to any Indian philosopher.

You cannot get to mind as an ultimate product of matter, for in the very attempt to do so you have already begun with mind. The earliest step of any such inquiry involves categories of thought, and it is in terms of

[1] Followers of the Vedas.

thought that the very problem you are investigating can be so much as stated. You cannot start in your investigations with bare, self-identical, objective facts, stripped of every ideal element or contribution from thought. The least and lowest fact of outward observation is not an independent entity-fact minus mind, and out of which mind may somehow or other be seen to emerge; but it is a fact or object *as it appears to an observing mind,* in the medium of thought, and having mind as an inseparable factor of it.[1]

So writes the Scotch philosopher in answer to modern materialistic theories of the universe, but it was impossible that the Vedanta school should have used this argument, for to have done so would have forced them to admit that the universe is a "fact as it appears to an observing mind," *i. e.*, to Brahma. But this was impossible, because, in the first place, to predicate observation of Brahma was to make him partaker of the "Illusion" of personality, and then where would escape lie? Or, if they escaped that horror, at least they made him responsible for matter, and so the cause of all the evils of life which they believed to flow from matter. To use such an argument presupposes an acceptance of the fundamental postulates of Christian thought: first, that "God saw everything that he had made and behold it was very good;" and the second, that "there is nothing either good or bad but *thinking* makes it so," *i. e.*, that all the evil of life takes its rise in a rebellious will.

It seemed, therefore, as if the Vedantists must

[1] *Philosophy of Religion,* Caird, p. 95.

either accept the dogma of Kapila, that intelligence is the offspring of matter, or else declare in favor of a sort of dualism. This they did before long, and found themselves involved in all the contradictions which are sure to flow from such a source.

This, then, was the Vedantan solution of the problem of life. At the centre of all life sits Brahma. But from all eternity he has been enveloped in a cloud of "Illusion." Out of that Illusion he has formed all things that are seen. It is true that it seems to us as if the things that are seen had reality, but that is because we partake so largely of the Illusion that we are not able to free our minds from its effects. The result of absorption into Brahma will be that we shall see things as they are. We are now like men who walk at night and, seeing a rope, mistake it for a snake. Their terror is groundless, but at the same time it is inevitable. Till the light of Brahma comes we shall be subject to fear, but in that light we shall see that that which we feared had no existence. Nothing is so deceptive as the senses. The very objects of them are in a state of perpetual flux. That which we predicate of phenomena to-day is inapplicable to-morrow. The rolling sun and gliding moon and heaving sea and trembling earth speak only of instability. There is no reality save the unseen life, of which nature is but the waving garment.

Professor Max Müller is never tired of calling our attention to the proof of kinship between the Germanic and the Indian peoples to be found in the common root from which the words "father," "mother," "daughter," and "home" have sprung. But I think we may find a stronger proof of the oneness of the human race in these old discussions by the banks of the Ganges which sound so modern. Then as now the men who walked by faith asked whence come the thoughts which witness to a home unseen, eternal, of the human soul. Then as now they had to meet the dogmatism of materialism, which simply asserted that all which has not its origin in sensation is illusion. It is not without comfort either to remember the teachings of Kapila, and note how little influence they had on the human race.

It may seem as if the philosophy of Kapila, which led to atheism and nihilism was the logical outcome of Indian philosophy, but it is not true, for though there is a certain philosophical connection between these various schools of thought, a glance at the history of Brahmanism is enough to show us how it is that men came to be atheists. Atheism then, as now, was not the revolt from spiritualism, but from ritualism. God the spirit must be worshiped in spirit. Any attempt to substitute ceremonialism for this worship leads to atheism, for atheism is the natural follower of materialism, and ceremonialism is materialism. If there be one thing more than another that the history of religion shows us, it is that when men have insisted that God must be worshiped in any special mountain, in any special way, there have not been wanting voices to assert that such a God is no God at all. That God is a spirit, and that they that worship Him must worship Him in "spirit and in truth," the human race has been witnessing to by its atheism more truly than by its ritualism. The only ground on which ritualism can be justified, apart from the question of individual edification, is, that it pleases God. Of course that leads at once to a consideration of the *character* of God. Now, if any age knows all that can be known of that character, it is well to embody that consciousness in ritual; but if there be a progress in that revelation, it is important that it be not so embodied, as a rite is difficult to change without a revolution. And inasmuch as the supposition is that ritual is the final statement of truth, this revolution is apt to lead to disbelief in the truth, *i. e.*, in God. That this is the state of affairs in Roman Catholic countries is notorious. The same effects followed a like cause in India.

Ceremonialism continued to be the way for the multitude, but the intellectual life of India flowed on between the two banks of materialistic atheism and idealistic pantheism, sometimes colored by one and sometimes by the other. But the great current of human life flowed on, unconscious of either. Scholars might dispute, but the common people had to live. But over life there lay a shadow. Beside the patient oxen there walked an unseen presence. Under the palm-trees there came a dream of endless rest; through the jungle there came at evening the whisper of an unknown tongue. The dying child opened his eyes with a startled look of recognition and fell back into the darkness that lies just outside of life. There was One among them they knew not. Was He friend or foe? No one could tell;

and so the common people crept to the temple door and cast in a handful of rice, or placed a wreath of yellow flowers on the shrine, and brought the infant son and laid him down at the idol's feet. If the unseen was a friend, he would be glad to be remembered. If he was a foe, perchance he would remember the child who had been brought with an offering, and pass him over when the other first-born fell.

No one can study the history of India as it was six hundred years before Christ without being struck with the resemblance to European history just before the Reformation. By the Ganges and by the Seine, at the foot of the Himalayas and in the valleys of the Alps, Nominalist and Realist disputed, and the common people stretched out their hands for God. In both periods men had reached a point where there must come a reformation or religion would die of its own inanity. In both periods the reformer came with a gospel to the poor.

CHAPTER V.

BUDDHISM.

Our examination of Indian thought has brought us to its culmination in the nihilism of Buddhism; but when we speak of Buddhism, it becomes necessary to define the limits of our subject, for the field is immense. The literature of Buddhism already makes a library and is increasing every day; the controversies concerning its fundamental doctrines bid fair to rival Christian theology. Then, again, it is divided into two great churches, the Northern and Southern, as unlike as Catholicism and Protestantism. The disciples of the latter are found in Ceylon, Burmah, and Siam; of the former, in Nepaul, Thibet, China, and Japan; also in Corea, though a recent traveler informs us, that Buddhism as an ecclesiastical system is, owing to political reasons, not found there. So that when one is speaking of Buddhism, it is as important to know whether he has in mind "The Great Vehicle" (as the Northern is called), or the "Little Vehicle," as its opponents contemptuously term the canon of the southern church.

Again, Buddhism as it exists in Thibet, with its splendid ritual and august hierarchy, with the Grand Lama at its head, is no more like what we may call the Congregational Buddhism in Japan, with its thirty-three sects, than the Papal court of Paul V. was like the Pilgrim band that gathered in prayer about Plymouth Rock. Of all religions, Buddhism is the one which has shown itself most susceptible to local influences. Mahometanism, though it too has its great schism, is practically the same in the palace of Persia and in the tents of Arabia; but Chinese Buddhism is not like Nepaulese, and Singhalese Buddhism differs from the religion of Burmah.

Again, Buddhism means to some minds a profound system of philosophy and science; to others an elaborate system of ritual; to others again, a debased idol worship; while a popular impression is gaining ground just now that what is called "esoteric" Buddhism is the only true form of the doctrine of Gautama; the representatives of which are the modern Yogin of India, the magicians who have become independent of the laws of nature. Now, undoubtedly, all these systems are in a sense related to the teaching of Gautama, but interesting as their study may be, they will not teach us what Buddhism is; indeed we cannot understand them unless we have learned the fundamental dogmas of Buddhism, and that can only be done by resorting to those teachings of the Great Master and his earliest disciples which all Buddhists acknowledge. If from these we can learn what Buddha taught concerning the Skandhas, Karman, and Nirvâna, we shall have the key to Buddhism, just as he who has learned the meaning of the Incarnation, the Cross, and the Resurrection has the key to Christian theology. The world has seen but three Catholic religions, and they are all the expression of the thought of a person, Buddhism, Mahometanism, and Christianity, and the secret of each is hidden in the life of its founder. We need then to glance first at the life of the Buddha.

About 600 years before Christ, there was born in the kingdom of Kapilavastu, now the province of Oudh, a prince, whose name Siddârtha has almost been lost sight of in the light of those titles which have been given to express the splendor of his noble life. The first of these was Gautama, which means the ascetic of the Gotamides. A second is Sâkyamouni, meaning the solitary one among the Sâkyas, — the name of the tribe to which he belonged. But the name most familiar to us is Buddha the enlightened one, — the name which one third of the human family pronounce with reverence as they turn their faces to the better life. It is the expression of the highest idea of life among the Aryans, as the word Christ was amongst the Hebrews. To be the anointed man of God was to the Jew the consummation of life. To be the enlightened one, to look with unfaltering eye on the light of life, seemed to the Hindu eternal peace. The Buddha is no rival of the Christ, but when we once know his life we are constrained to say that the words of Jesus concerning John the Baptist in his relation to the prophets of Israel is true of this man in his relation to the other Masters of Humanity. "Of all that are born of women there hath not arisen a greater" than Gautama, Sâkyamouni, Buddha.

Fancy has been busy here as elsewhere in weaving a coat of many colors for the infancy of this mighty man, but through the legendary mist we seem to see a simple-minded, pure, earnest boy growing up amidst the luxury and frivolity and flattery of an Oriental court, the wonder of his teachers, a mystery to the good king, his father, who, like the father of a greater one, sought him and sorrowed because he found him not amongst the ambitious of his kinsfolk and acquaintance, and wist not that the earnest lad was about his father's business.

The life moves on amid Oriental scenery. Before the young prince there come at the father's command all the beauty of the land; they pass by unnoticed till at last that life, which the Buddha afterwards said, with such a deep meaning, that he had known and loved in many a previous existence, stands before him; then the sleeping heart awakes with a bound, and the dreamy prince stands forth a man after his father's own heart, and gladly enters the lists to tame the unbroken steed, to throw the unconquered wrestler, to draw the unbending bow, that he may win the princess who has waked him to the joy of life.

For a moment the father's cup is full; no fault of his if the son do not remain to the end lapped in luxury, soothed with soft music, breathing sweet perfumes. From the harem the noiseless slaves carry the sick girl who may not cry out, on pain of death, lest the prince learn that life has sorrow; from the bush the fading rose leaf is picked in the early morning, lest the waking prince see that decay is the end of beauty; golden gates shut in the palace, lest the prince see that there is disease and death outside. But no slave can stop the wind which bloweth where it listeth, and it speaks to the kingly soul of other lands from whence it blows. The Western gates cannot prevent the sun's rays from pointing to other lands to which it stoops. Are all men happy there as is the prince with his gentle bride? Are all men happy just outside the gates? The prince will see.

The troubled father commands that when the prince goes through the town all shall seem bright and fair. So it is. But when the prince, happy at the sight of all the simple joy of his people, would turn back again to his own delights, then

<pre>
                          when midway in the road,
    Slow tottering from the hovel where he hid,
    Crept forth a wretch in rags, haggard and foul,
    An old, old man, whose shriveled skin, sun-tanned,
    Clung like a beast's hide to his fleshless bones.
    Bent was his back with load of many days!
    His eyepits red with rust of ancient tears,
    His dim orbs blear with rheum, his toothless jaws
    Wagging with palsy and the fright to see
    So many and such joy. One skinny hand
    Clutched a worn staff to prop his quavering limbs,
    And one was pressed upon the ridge of ribs,
    Whence came in gasps the heavy painful breath.
  "Alms," moaned he, "give good people! for I die
    To-morrow or the next day!" then the cough
    Choked him, but still he stretched his palm, and stood
    Blinking and groaning 'mid his spasms, "Alms!"
    Then those around had wrenched his feeble feet
    Aside, and thrust him from the road again,
    Saying, "The Prince! dost see? get to thy lair!"
    But that Siddârtha cried, "Let be! let be!
</pre>

Channa! what thing is this that seems a man,
Yet surely only seems, being so bowed,
So miserable, so horrible, so sad?
Are men born sometimes thus? What meaneth he
Moaning 'to-morrow or next day I die?'
Finds he no food that so his bones jut forth?
What woe hath happened to this piteous one?"
Then answer made the charioteer, "Sweet Prince!
This is no other than an aged man.
Some fourscore years ago his back was straight,
His eye bright, and his body goodly; now
The thievish years have sucked his sap away,
Pillaged his strength, and filched his will and wit;
His lamp has lost its oil, the wick burns black;
What life he keeps is one poor lingering spark
Which flickers for the finish: such is age;
Why should your Highness heed?" Then spake the Prince,
"But shall this come to others, or to all,
Or is it rare that one should be as he?"
"Most noble," answered Channa, "even as he
Will all these grow if they shall live so long."
"But," quoth the Prince, "if I shall live as long,
Shall I be thus; and if Yasodhara
Live fourscore years, is this old age for her,
Jalini, little Hasta, Gautami,
And Gunga, and the others?" "Yea, great Sir!"
The charioteer replied. Then spake the Prince:
"Turn back, and drive me to my house again!
I have seen that I did not think to see."

This then was what life might be. Again they go forth and see what must be the end of every life. What is the end of the lives of the sorrowful, asks the Prince.

"They die"
          "Die?"
                    "Yea, at the last comes death,
In whatsoever way, whatever hour.
Some few grow old, most suffer and fall sick,

But all must die — behold where comes the dead!"
Then did Siddârtha raise his eyes, and see
Fast pacing towards the river bank a band
Of wailing people, foremost one who swung
An earthen bowl with lighted coals, behind
The kinsmen shorn, with mourning marks, ungirt
Crying aloud, "O Rama, Rama, hear!
Call upon Rama brothers;" next the bier,
Knit of four poles with bamboos interlaced,
Whereon lay stark and stiff, with feet foremost, lean,
Chapfallen, sightless, hollow-flanked a-grin,
Sprinkled with red and yellow dust the Dead.

. . . .

Then spake the Prince: —

"Is this the end which comes to all who live?"
"This is the end that comes
To all," quoth Channa.

. . . .

"The high, the low, the good, the bad, must die,
And then, 't is taught, begin anew and live
Somewhere, somehow, — who knows? — and so again
The pangs, the parting and the lighted pile: —
Such is man's round."

Then the Prince : —

The vail is rent
Which blinded me! I am as all these men
Who cry upon the Gods and are not heard
Or are not heeded — yet there must be aid!
For them and me and all there must be help!
Perchance the gods have need of help themselves
Being so feeble that when sad lips cry
They cannot save! I would not let one cry
Whom I could save! How can it be that Brahm
Would make a world and keep it miserable,
Since, if all-powerful, he leaves it so
He is not good, and if not powerful,
He is not God? — Channa! lead home again!
It is enough! Mine eyes have seen enough!"[1]

[1] *The Light of Asia*, Book Third.

I have quoted at great length from "The Light of Asia," which has told the story of Buddha's life with great beauty and power, but I do not see how the crisis of his life could be better described than in the words of one of his disciples who has said, with the brief simplicity of our own Evangelists, "He was seized with a great compassion for this great multitude plunged in uncertainty."

That night the sun left him in his princely state, next morning it rose on him far from home, dressed in the yellow robe of the mendicant, holding the beggar's bowl for alms, seeking, in the only way he knew, the "Kingdom of God and his Righteousness." Of only One can it be said with a deeper meaning by his disciples, "Though he were rich yet for our sakes he became poor."

The force of any character is to be measured by the amount of hostile power in the conditions of his life which he overcomes. We are so apt to dwell upon the disadvantages and hindrances of poverty, that we are in danger of overlooking the much greater dangers of luxury. But, of course, it is a greater proof of power to cast aside the luxury of the court and adopt a life of hardship than to begin with hardship and end with fame, for the tendency of adversity is to brace a healthy character, but each year of luxury relaxes the sinews of the soul. It was the greater test to which Buddha was subjected, and the "Great Renunciation" is to the Buddhist what the Cross is to the Christian.

Indeed, it was inevitable that the reformation of Brahmanism should begin with a renunciation, for in the nature of things it was impossible that God should choose, in India, as in Judea, "the foolish things of the world." The caste system had so permeated life that no peasant would have been heard had he ventured to preach. The reformation must begin by the calling of the "*Mighty and the Noble.*"

Out of the legends that cluster thick about Gautama life we learn that for years after the Great Renunciation the man lived in the jungle, and in the caves of the mountains, seeking through the ascetic miseries of the reputed holy men, the Rishis, and the Yogin, to attain to peace. But it was in vain, and he returned again to the habitations of men seeking to learn the truth. And it came to him, as it has always come to man, not as the result of a logical process of thought, not as the immediate reward of any definite act, but as a "peace that passeth all understanding," it finally filled his heart and mind.

It was at Gâya, the legend says, sitting under the Bô tree, after long meditation, that deliverance came. As he sat silent, there rolled over his soul the successive waves of light. First he saw as from a mountain peak the successive stages of lives through which he had past, then came the insight into all that was to come, then he saw the secret of sorrow and the way of escape, where man

> glides —
> Lifeless — to nameless quiet, nameless joy,
> Blessed Nirvâna — sinless, stirless rest,
> That change which never changes.

The victory had been won, the seeker after truth had become enlightened. He was Buddha.

There is a popular impression that Buddha beginning *de novo* formulated an elaborate system of philosophy. There could be no greater mistake. Buddha was above all things a practical man; for speculation as such he had no interest. The problem of his life was how to *live*. The Brahmans had, as we have already seen, an elaborate system of philosophy, but together with it went a complicated system of ritual by which the gods were to be influenced. Now when Sâkyamouni came to ponder over the problem of life, he perceived that if the philosophy of the Upanishads was true there was no need of the ritual. Nay, more, if it was true, it was true for the gods as well as for men. So Buddha did not deny the existence of the gods, he simply ignored them. He was not an atheist but an agnostic.

We have already spoken of the two schools of Brahmanic philosophy, — the Sânkhya and the Vedanta. At the time of Buddha's Great Renunciation, they differed in little save in name. Buddha stood at the meeting of these two streams of thought. From his day they have formed one river. The Materialism of the Sânkhya school and the Pantheism of the Vedanta became at their junction the philosophy of Buddhism, what we may call an *idealized materialism*.

But the times were ripe for Buddhism, not only philosophically but also ecclesiastically. We have seen that the original scripture of the Indian Aryans was the Rig-Veda, and then that to this was added the Yagur and the Sama Vedas. The next step was to insert the Brahmanas in the canon, and then the

Upanishads followed. But no sooner had the various schools of thought arisen than a philosophic literature was produced, which began to have an influence upon the thinking portion of the community greater than that of the Vedas themselves. The consequence was that the adherents of one of the schools, probably the Mimansa, endeavored to have their Sûtras, as these writings were called, inserted as a part of the canon, on the ground that they embodied the "traditions of the fathers." Then began the great controversy concerning the Smriti and the Sûtri, that is, tradition and revelation. It was like the discussion in Europe concerning the false decretals, and the result in both cases was the same, a profound skepticism of the whole system founded on these traditions. At the height of this skeptical tide Buddha appeared.

The life of Gautama after his attainment to Buddhahood differed in no respect from that of the other teachers of his time, that is, he went throughout the land preaching the good news to those who had "ears to hear," and so, little by little, gathering about him a company of disciples. During the rainy season he rested in some quiet village; at the end of that season he spoke to the multitudes that flocked to hear him when it was known that he was in the neighborhood. Brahmans came with their disciples and tried to put him to silence, but could not withstand the wisdom and power with which he spake. Poor wretched outcasts crept to his side and learned how the thirst of lust might be quenched. The "great multitude plunged in uncertainty" found in him one who could teach them the true way of escape.

The method of his teaching was probably entirely unconventional, but his disciples soon formulated his sayings into a definite system of logical exactness. It consisted first of the "Four Noble Truths," which are: 1. The existence of pain. 2. The cause of pain. 3. The "Way" to the cessation of pain; 4. and then the end of all, Nirvâna. To appreciate the power of this teaching it is necessary to examine each of these truths in turn.

1. "The existence of pain." That need not detain us long. It is a fact which is as familiar to us as to the Buddha; it is one of the great cords that bind all living creatures together. I shall have something to say later of this as a starting-point of religion or philosophy; at present I merely wish to call attention to the fact. There is one thing to be remembered, however, before we pass on, and that is, that the existence of pain is much more apparent in the East than in the West. We hide our trouble and go through life as if we were happy whether we are or not. The Oriental at best only maintains a dignified silence. We hide our wounds, and house the sick, and cover the dead. In the East the leper lies on the bridge with his decaying limbs exposed to the gaze of every passer-by. The blind grope their way from house to house. The dead with uncovered face are carried along the highway on which the bride is being borne to the bridegroom's house.

The evidences of suffering are on every hand. So we can see why Buddha should have begun with sorrow. On the other hand, when we remember that the continual sight of suffering tends to deaden the sensibilities, we shall have a deeper appreciation of the loving heart of the noble prince whose only thought was of saving of the world from woe. "This, O monks, is the sacred truth of suffering: Birth is suffering, old age is suffering, sickness is suffering, death is suffering, to be united with the unloved is suffering, to be separated from the loved is suffering, not to obtain what one desires is suffering, in short the fivefold clinging to the earthly is suffering."[1] Nor was this all: to the Hindu, death and birth were alike in this, that both led only to sorrow: for birth leads to disease, and disease to decay, and decay to death, and death again to re-birth. To deliver man then from sorrow was to deliver him from the endless chain of existence.

2. What is the cause of sorrow? The answer to that question was the great discovery of the Buddha. It is Desire, more literally Thirst.

The thirst of thoughtless man grows like a creeper. He runs from life to life like a monkey seeking fruit in the forest.

Whomsoever this fierce thirst overcomes, full of poison in this world, his sufferings increase like the abounding Birâna grass.

He who overcomes this fierce thirst, difficult to be overcome in this world, sufferings fall off from him like waterdrops from a lotus leaf.[2]

Such was life, — a snare and a delusion. "Vanity of vanities" was not, as in the Hebrew Scriptures,

[1] Oldenburg's *Life of Buddha* (Eng. trans.), 211.
[2] Dhammapada, chap. xxiv. *Sacred Books of the East*, vol. x.

a note which, sounding the discord of life, only serves to emphasize the eternal harmony of life; it was the very theme of Buddhism. Man clutched at riches, and seized care; he pampered the senses, and bred disease; he sought for knowledge, and engendered doubt; reaching forth with his affections to embrace some life, it was snatched away. As death drew near, wishing ardently for a new life which would satisfy the unsatisfied cravings of this life, he bound himself still tighter to the fast revolving wheel of existence; the swifter its course the more desperately he clings to the engine of his destruction. So life is one endless horror, anguish, and despair! But how is this thirst to be quenched? In the first place the cause of the thirst must be discovered.

It would seem that the fear of making this plain to the world caused the Buddha to hesitate before proclaiming the Great Deliverance to men, and of that scheme no part seemed to him so difficult to make men understand as this cause of thirst. It is no wonder, for it will be difficult to say exactly what it means; at the same time we may well believe that the words had a meaning to the Hindu which we are unable to grasp. And another thing is to be borne in mind and that is, that often they did not care, in their dreamy mysticism, to attach any very definite meaning to the terms of a proposition if the general tenor of it commended itself to their feeling. If we look for a moment at the result of thirst we shall be able to see why, if that were extinguished, both its cause and effect ceased. The *result* of thirst is *clinging* to existence; the result of clinging is *birth*, from birth come *old age, pain, death*, and, if thirst still continues, *re-birth*. The constant metaphor which explained this was the flame of a candle. Man's life is the flame. As the fuel is consumed, the flame flickers to its extinction, but if a breath of wind *blows upon it* it will attach itself to new fuel. Now the wind which blows man's life is desire, thirst, lust. So if thirst can be extinguished the effects which are so disastrous will fail. Now look backward. Thirst arises from *sensation*, sensation results from *contact* between the senses and objects; the cause of this sensible contact, of course, is the *senses*. So far all is clear enough; but the senses result from *name* and *bodily form* (that is, I suppose, sentient being, which is true, but only states the cause in another denomination of the effect). Name and form result from *consciousness* (here I think we have a trace of the Sânkhya belief in the existence of innumerable individual souls as opposed to the Vedanta belief in the One Soul, Âtman). Individual consciousness is the result of the *Skandhas*, and the Skandhas are themselves the result of *Ignorance*. This last is the most obscure point of all, but very likely it points to the Vedanta belief in Maya, or the illusion which existed along with Brahma, and from which all that is seen is made, this being often spoken of as Ignorance. So if we do not scrutinize the terms too closely we shall be able to see how the destruction of this thirst will lead, by many steps, to the cessation of being and consequently of suffering. Thirst is the key-stone of the

Buddhist doctrine; remove that and the whole arch falls to the ground. Buddha desired nothing less; he was a nihilist. But his nihilism looked to something more than destruction; that was only a means to an end, which was the building of a better life on the ruins of the old.

These things, then, ignorance, consciousness, etc., are the fetters which bind the soul to life. They could have no power over man were it not that he lusts after them.

It is not ignorance that is to be dreaded, it is the *lust* of ignorance, the *desire* for consciousness, etc., which causes the misery of life. Man, therefore, has his fate in his own hands; he must be his own savior. "Quench this thirst and sorrow will fall off like water-drops from a lotus leaf."

3. But how is it to be quenched? The answer is by entering upon the noble path, — the way of salvation which the Buddha came to preach.

This path is eightfold; namely, right views, right aspirations, right speech, right conduct, right livelihood, right effort, right mindfulness, and right contemplation.[1]

Again the noble path is divided into four stages, each of which has its own appropriate blessing. The unconverted man is he who has not begun to walk the noble path; he is the slave of delusion. But he who has been converted is gradually freed from the three fetters, namely, the delusion of self, doubt concerning the Buddha, and belief in the efficacy of rites

---

[1] *Sacred Books of the East*, vol. xi.

and ceremonies. Freedom from these fetters is the fruit of the first stage.

The second stage is reached by those who, freed from the fetters, have reduced *sensuality*, *ill-will*, and *foolishness*. Such will return to this earth but once after death.

The third stage is reached by those who have utterly destroyed sensuality and ill-will. Free from all carnal affections and every evil thought they will return to the earth no more.

The last stage, only the worthy — the Arahats — attain to. These are they who have quenched all desire for life, all pride, all self-righteousness, all ignorance. Free from all delusion and sin, they see things only as they are. Having quenched all evil desire they are filled with pity and love for others.

To be in that state is to reach Nirvâna.[1]

To appreciate the value of this scheme of salvation it is necessary to bear in mind what it replaced.

At the time of Buddha there were but two ways of escape, — the one through sensuality, from which the Buddha shrunk as leading only to greater misery; and the path of asceticism, which the Buddha saw was impotent to bring peace to the soul.

There are two extremes, O Bhikkhus, which the man who has given up the world ought not to follow: the habitual practice, on the one hand, of those things whose attraction depends upon the passions, and especially of sensuality, — a low and pagan way of seeking satisfac-

[1] *Contemporary Review*, January, 1877, Buddhism, by Rhys Davids.

tion unworthy, unprofitable, and fit only for the worldly minded; and the habitual practice, on the other hand, of asceticism, — which is painful, unworthy, and unprofitable. There is a middle path, O Bhikkhus, . . . a path which opens the eyes and bestows understanding, which leads to peace of mind, to the higher wisdom, to full enlightenment; to Nirvâna![1]

This middle path is the way already described.

Now there can be no doubt that this was a veritable discovery of the great moral law that peace can be obtained only through righteousness. But righteousness means right relation, and there was no God with whom man was to be brought into right relation, — for while, as we have said before, Buddha did not deny the existence of the gods, he ignored them; they might exist, but in that case they needed to enter on the noble path as much as men. So the only righteousness was that between man and man and the man with himself,— that is, a sort of internal harmony. Another discovery, that the cause of all the misery of life is selfishness, was the work of Buddha. For when we look at it closely we see that the thirst which he so much deprecated was what we call selfishness. But, having no god, he could have no place for redemption in his scheme of salvation! All that he could promise was the extinction of the fires of passion.

Now wherein lay the power of this gospel? for that it has been a power in the history of the human race no one can deny. Rising out of the ruins of Brahmanism it overspread India and Ceylon. It

[1] *Sacred Books of the East*, vol. xi.

passed into Nepaul, and from thence, having undergone some modification, it developed a missionary spirit which led to triumphs in Thibet, China, Corea, and Japan. From Ceylon it passed to Burmah and Siam. Though it has been driven from India proper, being found only in Ceylon and Nepaul, yet modern Hinduism is a mixture of Buddhism and Brahmanism, while *Janism*, the religion of the Sikhs, is the result of a deliberate attempt to harmonize the two; so that while Buddhism has passed from India as Christianity did from Palestine, yet its influence is felt there still.

But its missionary spirit is not the most remarkable thing about it, still less will it account for its triumphs; for while zeal is a necessary element in missionary work, the important thing is always the cause of the zeal.

It has been supposed that it was the pure morality of Buddhism which kindled the enthusiasm of preacher and hearer, and undoubtedly there is much truth in that. The morality of Buddhism is so incomparably higher than anything that had preceded it in the East that it must have carried in itself the power of drawing sinful souls. Yet when we consider what human nature is, we shall feel convinced that what the human race wants is not *goodness*, but happiness. As with the child, so with the race; it requires a long course of education before it can identify happiness with goodness. The time does come when men can turn away from apparent happiness with the absolute certainty that eternal happiness is found only by those who find their satisfaction in drinking at the fountain of goodness. Now when we remember that eighteen centuries of Christianity have not sufficed to convince all men who have come under its influence of this truth, and are told that Hindus, Singhalese, Burmese, Siamese, and Chinese welcomed Buddhism because of its pure morality, we may well be skeptical!

Buddha, then, must have had some good news, some gospel. What was it?

There are three ways in which the attainment of happiness may be presented to men. The first is the heathen way. "Do something that your god likes, sacrifice a bullock or a goat, or, better still, your firstborn child, and he will pay you." The second is the Buddhist. "Walk in the Noble Path of virtue, and you will *earn* happiness," as the reward. The third is the Christian. "The free gift of God is eternal life in Christ Jesus our Lord."

The first is perfectly arbitrary; there is no necessary connection between the offering of a beast and the divine favor. It may be bought at a fixed price. Buddhism repudiated that, and said there is a necessary connection between righteousness and happiness. Do right and you will earn it. It was an immense advance on heathenism. It was a veritable discovery of the eternal law. But there is something higher still, and that is the offering to every soul eternal life, that is the awakening of the soul to the conscious realization of its life being hidden with Christ in God, which will *manifest itself* in righteousness. Freedom from sin, peace with God, and joy in the Spirit of Holiness.

The success of Buddhism may in part be accounted for by its missionary zeal, and by its method of attaining happiness which appealed to a higher instinct of the human race. But what was the happiness it proposed? The happiness of heathenism was intelligible enough. The god will not destroy your cattle with hailstones. When you die he will save you from torment.

The happiness of the Christian is appreciable; it is the gaining of a new spirit, the spirit of power, the spirit of joy, and the spirit of peace.

Now what was the happiness of Buddhism? It was Nirvâna. What that was we may be able to say later. This much we can say, that it was deliverance from existence in any such form as we know it now. Sad as it may seem, that was the cause of the triumph of Buddhism. The pessimism of the East had permeated every crevice of life, until men had lost interest in living. It has been well said that no more horrible message could be imagined by the Oriental than that life is everlasting. The causes of this pessimism it is impossible here to discuss. Undoubtedly it is partly physical. A man whose life is hardly kept from ebbing away by a handful of rice can feel no thrill in simply living, as did the strong limbed Greek! A social system which killed all hope for the individual as well as for the family made long life — that glory of the Hebrew — a horror to the Hindu. A philosophy which restrained the desire to die by the fear of a re-birth after death made men "rather bear the ills they had than fly to others which they knew not of." These were some, if not all, of the causes of a pessimism that so colored all life, that escape from it into an inexperienced and yet still in some dull way hoped for peace came to them as a veritable gospel, — a good news.

Yet it was not annihilation that Buddha promised his disciples, at least not immediately upon death — if ever. Why he should not have done so is one of those inconsistencies which are the glory of a truly religious soul. Why had he who had cut himself loose from the popular theology, who had risen to the knowledge of the power of the law of righteousness, why did not he go a step further and discard the belief in the transmigration of souls, and say boldly, "The end of life is annihilation?" The answer is twofold: First, there was his firm conviction that the law of right was *eternal;* and then there was the Brahmanic philosophy in which he had been trained. A man cannot entirely rid himself of his past any more than he can outstrip his own shadow, and Buddha was no exception to the rule.

The legend of Buddha declares that it was the sight of suffering which caused Buddha to renounce the pleasures of life and begin the life of a preacher of salvation to a sorrowful world. But it has been well said that we may be sure that this effect was caused not by that sight alone, but by a painful sight on a mind already saddened by the collapse of some ideal. It was the collapse of the popular philosophy which led Buddha and his first disciples to enter upon the "Noble Path."

There are three points in that philosophy which we must consider if we would understand the teaching of Buddha.

The first is what is called the doctrine of the " Skandhas" or Groups. Both schools of philosophy, that is the Sankhya and the Vedanta, began with the doctrine of the Skandhas, that is to say, they both denied the proper individuality of man. According to the Sankhya school the individuality of man was due to the union of an eternally preëxistent independent soul with matter,[1] in which term they included material qualities, sensations, abstract ideas, the natural tendencies or disposition of the life and thought, or reason. Now from the junction of these groups with the preëxistent soul was produced the individuality, just as by the mixture of two or more chemical elements is produced a gas which did not reside in either of them alone. When it is added that the soul was dependent for "consciousness"[2] upon this incarnation, we shall see that the Sankhya doctrine was pure materialism.

But the Indian mind has always shrunk from materialism, because it leads to Atheism, and it is saturated with Theism. Nevertheless, there were some who boldly announced the conclusion to which their philosophy led, and declared that on the dissolution of the Skandhas, that is at death, the soul ceased to be; that the result of death is annihilation.[3]

The Vedanta doctrine differed from the foregoing in its denial of the separate existence of individual souls, and consequently in its rejection of the doc-

---

[1] Barth's *Religions of India* (Eng. trans.), p. 70.
[2] See *Indian Wisdom*, p. 96.
[3] See Oldenburg's *Life of Buddha* (Eng. trans.), p. 273, *note*.

trine of the necessity of the Skandhas for consciousness. Both agreed that on the dissolution of the Skandhas the soul was set free, but the Vedanta taught that it returned to the source of all life, the one soul, the Âtman of the universe.

What now was Buddha's relation to this doctrine? There is no doubt that he was most in sympathy with the extreme Sankhya teaching. But he differed from it in two respects: in the first place he did not believe in preëxistent eternal souls; he believed that the soul is the result of the junction of the Skandhas. He subdivided them till they included every variety of sensation and imagination. He did not go back of this doctrine. He accepted and developed it A favorite illustration was this: You see something which you call a chariot. It consists of body, and wheels, and a pole. Divide them, take them all apart, you have not destroyed the elements, but you have destroyed the *chariot*.[1] In other words, the chariot was only a term given to express the relation of certain things to each other; it is a fiction; so is the soul. It has no existence apart from the Skandhas. So it was that the Buddha taught that the first of all delusions from which man must be delivered was the delusion of self. The vain imagination that he had any proper individuality apart from the conjunction of the Skandhas. This was what caused all the misery of life. The attempt to gain something from life that should be the possession of an individuality which had no real existence was as senseless as if a man

---

[1] Oldenburg's *Life of Buddha*, p. 256.

were to deny himself the necessaries of life that he may heap up riches for a child that is already dead. Yet this is what Buddha saw both schools of philosophy were encouraging men to do. It was their failure to bring peace that led to the Buddhist doctrine of the Skandhas.

So far, the doctrine of Buddha was only an amplification of the Sankhya school of philosophy, but here it seems to have been deflected from its logical path by the teaching of the Vedanta school. We have already seen that the Vedanta school accepted the doctrine of the Skandhas in a modified form : teaching, however, that the soul on the dissolution of the Skandhas was re-absorbed in the divine essence, but not immediately on death. Not until purified from all taint of corruption by passing through many stages of transmigration was the soul capable of that re-absorption which would end its miseries.

It was at this point that Buddha parted company with the Sankhya school, and followed the teachings of the Vedanta. He preached with a power never before equaled the doctrine of the transmigration of souls.

Now here is the puzzle : Why did he, who had rejected the dogma of a Supreme Being, not continue with the materialistic Sankhya school, and say the misery of the soul ends with death which dissolves the Skandhas ? Why did he suddenly turn to the idealistic Vedantism and accept the doctrine of the transmigration of souls ? I believe it was because his soul hungered and thirsted after righteousness.

The soul might be the result of the Skandhas, but if death ended all, then there was no answer to the awful moral problem of life; and so while we cannot affirm that Buddha believed in the immortality of the soul, yet he detained the soul, as it were, between heaven and earth, and insisted that it should give some answer to the moral problem of suffering.

The answer to that problem, and at the same time an incentive to virtue, Buddha found in the doctrine of Kamma. At first sight it would seem as if there were no distinction between the Brahmanic doctrine of the transmigration of souls and the Buddhist teaching of Kamma; the difference, however, is that Kamma was a highly developed form of the Brahmanic doctrine. The Brahmans taught, "An evil life will be punished by re-birth into a lower form of existence. A good life will be rewarded by a better life, and this will continue until the soul is sufficiently pure to be re-absorbed into Brahma." Now this doctrine of re-absorption in some sense underlay all Oriental teaching, — the object of such absorption being to destroy the individuality. The word Kamma, which means, literally, "act," had been used by the Brahmans to designate the ritual which was an "act" performed not only for men, but also for the gods. Upon this "act" gods and men were alike dependent. This prepared the way for Buddha; when he asked himself upon what gods and men were alike dependent, he answered that it could not be the senseless ceremonies, it must be some moral act. So with Buddha the "act," or Kamma of life, was that which resulted from the thirst for existence. Thus: here is a child; it has done in this life neither good nor bad, yet it has begun life deformed in body, or, still worse, in mind; or, even worse still, it came into this world with an almost irresistible tendency to lust or deeds of violence. How came it to be so? Calvinism has its answer, It is the manifestation of the divine wrath against sinful flesh. Modern science has its answer, It is the result of heredity. Buddha said it was Kamma. That is, when that life which is now in the child came to die in a previous life it clung to some evil, and the result of the clinging is the Kamma, or act, which we see now. The soul is like a flame which is dependent for its existence upon the fuel which it consumes; if it did not attach itself to new fuel it would not revive.[1] The child has not inherited a curse pronounced on the race; the child has not inherited the evil tendencies of its ancestors; the child has inherited its own evil tendencies; the child is its *own soul's parent!*[2]

It was this belief which prevented Buddha from accepting the materialistic theory of the annihilation of the soul at death, which we should have supposed must follow, naturally, from the belief that the soul is the result of the Skandhas. "When they dissolve the soul must cease to be," we would say, but not so Buddha; he said, "No, the soul is the result of the Skandhas it is true, but it has within itself the power of forming new Skandhas," which will remain

---

[1] Oldenburg's *Life of Buddha*, p. 262.
[2] *Contemporary Review*, January, 1877.

when the old have dissolved. But the thing that revived on the death of the old life, and created the identity between the two lives, was not self-consciousness, nor will, nor affection, but simply Kamma, the net result of the previous life. The suffering man and the sinner had no right to complain; they were simply reaping what they had sown.

According to Buddha every life was the slave of Kamma. If there were gods they were not free. He looked back over the long vista of life, and he saw the reckless sowing of tares; he looked about him, and he saw the harvest being gathered with tears. He looked into the future, and he saw the unending road that stretched itself before life. Birth, and death, and birth again, thirsting desire never quenched, bright hopes disappointed, — health sinking into disease, agony leading to death, and death to life, and so on forever, and ever, and ever. He looked above him, and heard of a Divine Essence that waited in dumb silence to absorb life, — and he turned in righteous indignation from such a God. He saw men crowd the temples, and he knew that like shipwrecked sailors they were drinking the salt water which could only serve to increase the madness of their thirst.

Then in the midst of that silent agony he heard the voice which had spoken to the Hebrew Psalmist, saying, "Keep innocency, and take heed unto the thing that is right, for that will bring a man peace at the last." So it was that he begun to preach his gospel, promising to all who entered on the Noble Path that they should be

> Released from all the skandhas of the flesh;
> Broken from ties — from Upâdânas — saved
> From whirling on the wheel; aroused and sane
> As is a man wakened from hateful dreams,
> Until, greater than kings, than gods more glad!
> The aching craze to live ends, and life glides —
> Lifeless — to nameless quiet, nameless joy,
> Blessed Nirvâna — sinless, stirless rest,
> That change which never changes.[1]

We can see then why the Buddha was hailed as a deliverer. It was because he promised freedom from that law of Kamma to which every Oriental believed himself to be subject. To the Western mind it is difficult to reach the point where it can appreciate the doctrines of the Skandhas and Kamma, but we must remember that with the Oriental they were ultimate facts of consciousness as truly as our *cogito ergo sum*. But when we reach this point the Noble Path stretches before as a straight road which we may follow to the end.

We have seen that the " path " was twelvefold, — eight right things and four stages; we have seen that the objective of the path was the destruction of thirst, but we have not found the secret of the path, that which gave force to it.

It was that which has given life to every religion since the world began; it was *faith*. The theory of Buddhism was that every man was to be his own savior, but it was impossible that this could be; and it was soon found that while the " poor " would follow a teacher, they could not apply a theory of salvation to their souls; and so we find that during the

[1] *The Light of Asia*, Book the Sixth.

lifetime of the Buddha a difficulty arose regarding the state of the faithful departed, and the Buddha answered: "Now there is nothing strange in this that a human being should die, but as each one does so you should come to the Buddha and inquire about them in this manner, that is wearisome to the Buddha. I will therefore teach you a way of truth, called the mirror of truth, which if an elect disciple possess he may himself predict of himself, 'Hell is destroyed for me, and re-birth as an animal, or a ghost, or in any other place of woe. I am converted, I am no longer liable to be re-born in a state of suffering, and am assured of final salvation.'"

"What, then, Ananda, is this mirror of truth? It is the consciousness that the elect disciple is in this world possessed of faith in the Buddha, believing the blessed one to be the holy one, the fully-enlightened one, wise, upright, happy, world-knowing, supreme, the bridler of men's wayward hearts, the teacher of gods and men, the blessed Buddha." [1] To this is added faith in the truth proclaimed by Buddha, and faith in the Church as the keeper of the truth.

This is as much as was expected of the great body of Buddhists, and soon took the place of the weightier matters of the law. The daily confession of faith is the great safeguard of the faithful. "I take my refuge in Buddha; I take refuge in the Law."

But for those who were able to bear it there was

[1] The Book of the Great Decease, chap. ii., *Sacred Books of the East*, vol. xi.

the more excellent way of moral exertion. But when we look into that we find that it too was modified to answer the needs of an indolent people. The eight right things are reduced to one, that is, right contemplation. Thus we read in the "Book of the Great Decease:" "Great is the fruit, great the advantage of earnest contemplation when set round with upright conduct. Great is the fruit, great the advantage of intellect when set round with earnest contemplation. The mind set round with intelligence is freed from the great evils, that is to say, from sensuality, from individuality, from delusion, and from ignorance." [1] Now in this passage we see that right conduct is dependent upon intelligence, and intelligence upon contemplation, but if we look at the passage in the same book on "Contemplation" we shall see that it ends in trance, and that intelligence is the power by which the mind prevents its excitation by sensible objects.

Now the stages of deliverance, Ananda, are eight in number. Which are the eight?

A man possessed with the idea of form sees forms; this is the first stage of deliverance.

Without the subjective idea of form, he sees forms externally; this is the second stage of deliverance.

With the thought it is well, he becomes intent upon what he sees; this is the third stage of deliverance.

By passing quite beyond all idea of form, by putting an end to all idea of resistance, by paying no attention to the idea of distinction, he, thinking it is all infinite space, reaches mentally and remains in the state of mind

[1] The Book of the Great Decease, chap. ii., *Sacred Books of the East*, vol. xi.

in which the idea of the infinity of space is the only idea that is present; this is the fourth stage of deliverance.

By passing quite beyond all idea of space being the infinite basis, he, thinking it is all infinite reason, reaches mentally and remains in the state of mind to which the infinity of reason is alone present; this is the fifth stage of deliverance.

By passing quite beyond the mere consciousness of the infinity of reason, he, thinking nothing at all exists, reaches mentally and remains in the state of mind to which nothing at all is specially present; this is the sixth stage of deliverance.

By passing quite beyond all idea of nothingness he reaches mentally and remains in the state of mind to which neither idea nor the absence of ideas are specially present; this is the seventh stage of deliverance.

By passing quite beyond the state of ideas or the absence of ideas he reaches mentally and remains in the state of mind in which both sensations and ideas have ceased to be; this is the eighth stage of deliverance.[1]

We see, then, to what it all led; it really was a return to the old Brahmanic theory of absorption through contemplation; the difference being that the Brahman expected a union with the Âtman as the result, while Buddha expected nothing but the extinction of the fires of passion and destructive thirst. Before we attempt an answer to the question as to the meaning of Nirvâna, which was to result from this extinction, let us run our eye over this plan of salvation again.

First, then there was the fundamental dogma,

[1] The Book of the Great Decease, chap. ii., *Sacred Books of the East*, vol. xi.

Life is misery: (1), because of evident pain and sorrow; and (2), because those things which are counted joys are delusions which end in sorrow.

Secondly. There is properly speaking no such thing as *individuality*. That which we speak of as the individual soul is not an entity, but only a mode of existence of certain physical, mental, and moral Skandhas; this, however, is not dissipated at the physical death, which dissolves the Skandhas, because the Kamma, that which the life has done, remains and forms the individuality of the new life, is the heir of all its tendencies, and the inheritor of all its sorrows.

Thirdly. There would be no Kamma, no "doing" by any life, were it not that back of this present life there is the pressure of an irresistible tendency or predisposition which arose in some previous existence, and an accursed thirst which leads the soul to drink of that which only begets desire. Destroy this thirst, break the chain of this tendency, and you are free.

Fourthly. This can be done only by entering on the Noble Path. The cause of desire is ignorance.[1] "If," said the Buddha, " you could see things as they are you would desire nothing." Who would stretch forth his hand to pluck a fruit if he knew an adder would bite him? There is an adder behind all fruit. He taught: —

> . . . how sorrow is
> Shadow to life, moving where life doth move;
> Not to be laid aside until one lays
> Living aside, with all its changing states,

[1] This seems to conflict with the statement above that "Desire" is the cause of all; but the Buddhist would answer, Ignorance is not the cause of desire, but the desire *for* ignorance!

> Birth, growth, decay, love, hatred, pleasure, pain,
> Being and doing. How that none strips off
> The sad delights and pleasant griefs who lacks
> Knowledge to know them snares, but he who knows
> *Avidya* — Delusion — *sets* those snares
> Loves life no longer but insures escape.[1]

Destroy the thirst and you no longer forge new links in the chain of existence. Destroy the "tendencies," and you break those which have been forged in the past. How can this be done? By doing right, and thinking right, and being right. Wrong doing, wrong thinking, wrong being produce, by a changeless law, an evil Kamma. As Jesus said, "Whoso committeth sin is the servant of sin." The Buddha taught that he who would do no evil would have no Kamma to revive, but would glide peaceful and calm into the unending bliss of Nirvâna, where no delusion deceives the weary soul, but where the aching craze to live ends, and life

> glides —
> Lifeless — to nameless quiet, nameless joy,
> Blessed Nirvâna — sinless, stirless rest,
> That change which never changes.

What now is meant by Nirvâna? The word means literally "not blown upon." It is a state of perfect calm. In it there is no more sorrow, for the soul is isolated, not in contact with any of the Skandhas. The evil power of Kamma broken, there is no more struggle. That which was capable of rebirth had died, there is no more fear. The penalty of all evil doing having been gathered home and patiently borne, there is no more sin.

[1] *Light of Asia*, Book the Sixth.

It is a state of enlightenment. Intelligence is not, as we should say, an act requiring observation and reflection. It is a wall of light which keeps the outer darkness from coming near the soul. "The mind set round with intelligence is freed from the great evils, that is to say, from sensuality, from individuality, from delusion, and from ignorance." Nirvâna is a peace "which passeth all understanding."

So far we can all go, but the question which concerns us most of all is this. Did Buddha preach annihilation? Is that the goal of the Noble Path? It would be most presumptuous in me to attempt to answer dogmatically a question which has divided the world of Oriental scholarship. I may, however, call your attention to one or two points in this discussion which may serve to guide our judgment in this most difficult path.

And the first thing to notice is that entrance into the state of Nirvâna is quite independent of the physical accident of death. If the Kamma is not exhausted Nirvâna is not attained at death, and when the state of supreme intelligence is reached Nirvâna is entered before death.

In the "Book of the Great Decease" the condition of the last disciple whom the Buddha received into the order is thus described.

So Subhadda, the mendicant, was received into the higher grade of the order under the Blesed One; and from immediately after his ordination the venerable Subhadda remained alone and separate, earnest, zealous, and resolved, and ere long he attained to that supreme goal of the higher life for the sake of which men go out from all and every household, gain and comfort, to become houseless wanderers, yea, that supreme goal did he by himself, and while yet in this visible world, bring himself to the knowledge of and continue to realize, and to see face to face!

Another thing that we have to notice is this, that Nirvâna is a condition of ecstasy rather than of unconsciousness.

In the "Book of the Great Decease" is this story.[1]

Now at that time a man named Pukkusa, a young Mallian, a disciple of Alara Kâlâma's, was passing along the high road. . . . And Pukkusa saw the Blessed One seated at the foot of a tree. On seeing him, he went up to the place where the Blessed One was, and when he had come there he saluted the Blessed One, and took his seat respectfully on one side. And when he was seated Pukkusa, the young Mallian, said to the Blessed One, "How wonderful a thing is it Lord! and how marvelous, that those who have gone forth out of the world should pass their time in a state of mind so calm!" Formerly, Lord, Alara Kâlâma was once walking along the high road; and leaving the road he sat down under a certain tree to rest during the heat of the day. Now, Lord, five hundred carts passed by one after the other, each close to Alara Kâlâma. And a certain man who was following close behind that caravan of carts went up to the place where Alara Kâlâma was, and when he came there he spoke as follows to Alara Kâlâma:—

"But, Lord, did you see those five hundred carts go by?"

"No, indeed, sir, I saw them not."

"But, Lord, did you hear the sound of them?"

"No, indeed, sir, I heard not their sound."

[1] xi. 75.

"But, Lord, were you then asleep?"

"No, sir, I was not asleep."

"But, Lord, were you then conscious?"

"Yes, I was conscious, sir."

"So that you, Lord, though you were both conscious and awake, neither saw nor heard the sound of five hundred carts passing by one after the other, and each close to you. Why, Lord, even your robe was sprinkled over with the dust of them!"

"It is even so, sir."

Then thought that man, "How wonderful a thing is it, and how marvelous, that those who have gone forth out of the world should pass their time in a state of mind so calm!"

And in this connection the Buddha told a story of his own experience more wonderful still.

Now on one occasion, Pukkusa, I was dwelling at Âtumâ, and was at the threshing-floor. At that time the falling rain began to beat and to splash, and the lightnings to flash forth, and the thunderbolts to crash; and two peasants, brothers, and four oxen were killed. Then, Pukkusa, a great multitude of people went forth from Âtumâ, and went up to the place where the two peasants, brothers, and the four oxen lay killed.

Now at that time, Pukkusa, I had gone forth from the threshing-floor, and was walking up and down *thinking* at the entrance to the threshing-floor. And a certain man came, Pukkusa, out of that great multitude of people, and when he came up he saluted me and took his place respectfully on one side.

And as he stood there, Pukkusa, I said to the man, "Why, then, sir, is this great multitude of people assembled together?" And he answered: —

"But, just now, the falling rain began to beat and to splash, and the lightnings to flash forth, and the thunderbolts to crash, and two peasants, brothers, were killed, and four oxen. Therefore is this great multitude gathered together. But where, Lord, were you?"

"I, sir, have been here all the while."

"But, Lord, did you see it?"

"I, sir, saw nothing."

"But, Lord, did you hear it?"

"I, sir, heard nothing."

"Were you, then, Lord, asleep?"

"I, sir, was not asleep."

"Were you, then, conscious, Lord?"

"Even so, sir."

Then, Pukkusa, the thought occurred to that man: "How wonderful a thing is it, and marvelous, that those who have gone forth out of the world should pass their time in a state of mind so calm!"

We see, then, that Nirvâna, so far from being a state of annihilation which the devout soul was to wish to reach after death, was a moral condition of freedom from passion which might be attained here. As Max Müller has said: "If we look in the Dhammapada, at every passage where Nirvâna is mentioned there is not one which would require that its meaning should be annihilation; while most, if not all, would become perfectly unintelligible if we assigned to the word Nirvâna that signification."

Or, as an equally high authority, Mr. Rhys Davids, has said: "It follows, I think, that, to the mind of the composer of the Buddhavansa, Nirvâna meant not the extinction of being, but the extinction of the three fires of passion."

But, it may be asked, how are we to account for
the fact that so many distinguished scholars[1] have
held a contrary opinion? How are we to interpret
such words as these,—which occur in the "Book
of the Great Decease": "And he became conscious that birth was at an end; that the higher life
had been fulfilled; that all that should be done had
been accomplished, and that after this present life
there *would be no beyond.*"[2]

I think the explanation of the paradox is this:
Buddha had been trained in an atmosphere of
thought which regarded *individuality* as a curse,
according to the Sankhya school, because it was a
delusion; according to the Vedanta, because true
happiness consisted only in union with the divine.

To Buddha neither explanation was satisfactory.
This was his: At the dissolution of the Skandhas,
that is at death, the individuality is not destroyed,
because Kamma remains, and that, taking the place
of individuality, forms the nucleus around which
new Skandhas form. So the Buddhists came to
speak of *Kamma* as the individuality, and hated it,
because it was the foundation of sentient life, which
is sorrow. When Kamma was destroyed individuality
was destroyed,—not consciousness, but self-will and
desire. All that remained to those who yet existing
had gone "out of the world" was the consciousness
of a victory won, and the exquisite languor of a soul
too weary to move and too content to wish,—"a

---

[1] Oldenburg claims to have found many passages in the Singhalese books which incline to the doctrine of annihilation.

[2] *Book of the Great Decease*, xi. 110.

sublime state of conscious rest in Omniscience." [1]
We are told distinctly that the Buddha was asked by his disciples what came after the last death. A soul has entered Nirvâna, yet the body has still to die. There is no Kamma to form a new individuality. Will, then, death destroy Nirvâna, — will the perfect peace end with death? And the Buddha would not answer. He said the question was not practical. I have no doubt he could not answer. But that need not surprise us. I believe if the same question had been put to Moses he would have said: " Eternal life is to know God. Whether eternal life is *everlasting* I do not know. Whether we live after death, as the Egyptians teach, I cannot tell. The question is not practical; our prayer should be, — 'So teach us to number our days, that we may apply our hearts unto wisdom.' "

In some such way the Buddha spake: —

> "No need hath such to live as ye name life,
> That which began in him when he began
> Is finished : He hath wrought the purpose through
> Of what did make him man.
>
> "Never shall yearnings torture him, nor sins
> Stain him, nor ache of earthly joys and woes
> Invade his safe, eternal peace : nor deaths
> And lives recur. He goes
>
> "Unto Nirvâna. He is one with Life
> Yet lives not. He is blest, ceasing to be.
> *Om Mani Padme,* Hum! The dew-drop slips
> Into the shining sea ! "

[1] It is important in this connection to remember the meaning of Nirvâna, which is, "not blown upon." Now as the object of the Buddhist was to prevent the flame of life being blown upon by *lust*, the goal would be reached as soon as lust was destroyed.

Such is Buddhism. The most fearless facing of the stupendous facts of life, the most heroic effort to attain unto righteousness, the most sublime proclamation that knowledge is eternal life, and the sweetest picture of the soul's rest that the world has ever seen apart from the life of Jesus. There are not wanting voices to tell us that it will be the religion of the future, but that will never be; for when all is said Buddhism still remains an Oriental religion. It is the pessimism of the Oriental mind oppressed by the magnitude of nature, and disgusted with itself, that forms the soil in which Buddhism can grow. It vanishes like a nightmare at the preaching of the redemption of the world by a greater man of sorrows than Gautama; yet, it has deep notes within it which find an echo in the human heart. To the busy man of affairs Buddha's "intelligence," a contemplation that is too deep for conscious differentiation, will seem unspeakably foolish; but to the religious soul, weary with glib definitions of great mysteries, it will not seem improbable that something like that will be found in the "Pavilion where there is the hiding from the strife of tongues."

But, after all, it is not Buddha's philosophy but Buddha who has been the power in the East. That great and noble personality towers above all religious life, at once a refuge and an inspiration.

If we ask for the secret of the Buddha's power, we must find it, as we do the secret of all power, in the fact that first of all he embodied in his life the Oriental ideal. The man who can do that is the great man — an Alexander, or a Napoleon; but he did more, and thus showed himself one of the greatest of men. He not only embodied the Oriental ideal of dignity, and contemplation, and asceticism; he elevated that ideal, and showed that dignity was compatible with fellowship with the pariah, that contemplation would sink to spiritual self-indulgence unless it was joined with works of mercy. He showed by his life that true asceticism consisted not in self-inflicted torture, but in the "fast from sin." It was in this way that he came nearest to Jesus. Jesus called himself the Son of David, but he soon enlarged that to the Son of *Man*. Can Jesus, then, answer the wants of the East as well as the demands of the West? Can he rouse the dreamy Oriental as well as inspire the energetic Occidental? Can he be to the Orient all that Buddha is and more? That is the question which we now must try to answer.

CHAPTER VI.

CHRIST'S RELIGION AND BUDDHISM.

No objection is more frequently urged against the religion of Christ, than that the stories, in the Gospels, of Jesus' childhood have been borrowed from earlier Oriental religious books. Even if this could be shown to be true it would not affect the truth of Christian revelation; for that is embodied in the character of Jesus, and that was the possession of the Church for fifty years, more or less, before the impression it made on the four Evangelists was *recorded.* So that to prove a particular story in any one of them to be an error does not affect the revelation; for the character of Jesus is a part of the heritage of humanity, dependent not upon the letter of the title-deed so much as upon the consciousness of the Church of its truthfulness. But indeed the objection will not bear an examination. It will be found in the first place that many of the Gospel stories have been adapted to Buddhist hearers; as for instance the story of Christ's interview with the Rabbis in the Temple. When it is said that the same story is related of Buddha, the first impulse may be to assert that the Gospel story is a copy. But look at the two. According to the Buddhist tradition the young prince shows himself master of all the learning of his teachers and able to instruct them. So that we read that one of his teachers fell prostrate before him and cried, "Thou art teacher of thy teachers." But when we look at the Gospel story, we read that Jesus went up to the Temple and *sat at the feet* of the doctors. With childlike faith He believed that the appointed teachers of the nation could answer the questions which had begun to stir his soul. He never dreamed of teaching them. The art that would picture Jesus as declaiming before the astonished Rabbis has missed the meaning of the story. This, then, is the difference: the one is the old story of the precocious childhood, and the other is the record of a child that was not precocious, but who gradually increased in wisdom and stature, in favor with God and man. A life that was perfectly *natural* because of its supernatural grasp upon all that was essentially human.

The story of Jesus learning from the doctors was never borrowed from Buddha's teaching of his teachers. The latter may be a copy of the Gospel story by one who had missed the meaning of the original. And indeed it is to be remembered that the contact of East and West has been nearer than has been supposed.

In one of the splendid Buddhist temples of Japan, there hangs a bell of very exquisite workmanship. Beside it stand two noble candelabra. The first impulse is to say that the altars and towers of Europe are decked with the spoils of the East, but a closer look will disclose a date of the seventeenth century, and a closer study will teach us that perhaps at the very time the Pilgrim Fathers were sojourning in Holland, staunch Protestant sailors were stealing bells and candelabra from the Catholic cathedrals of the Netherlands to decorate Buddhist temples in Japan! — a view of history which is startling, perhaps, but which may serve to save us from hasty generalizations concerning kindred traditions in Buddhist and Christian Scriptures.

A second point which must be noticed before beginning the consideration of the relation between Buddhist and Christian theology is Buddhist morality.

There are three points in Buddhist morality which it is said show a superiority over Christianity, inasmuch as the Buddhist morality was preached centuries before Christ, and the teachings of Christ do not, it is asserted, surpass it. Now even if this be true, it does not tell against Christianity; on the contrary, Jesus distinctly told his disciples that He came not to destroy, but to fulfill. So if the religion of Jesus be the religion for mankind, then it must fulfill not only the law of the Jew, but also all that the human heart responds to amongst the Gentiles.

Let us look, then, at the three great commandments of the Buddhist law. The first is the destruction of caste, the second the giving of alms, and the third the forgiveness of injuries.

And first, as regards the destruction of the caste system, there could no greater mistake than to suppose that it was an object of attack by Buddha. He simply preached deliverance for all who were oppressed by sorrow, and that gracious message no doubt drew many low caste men and women. But no sooner were they gathered together than a new caste was instituted. Those only could attain to Nirvâna who became ascetics. Now as that was impossible for the large majority of men, the disciples of Buddha were at once divided into two classes; those who sought the higher life, and those who, immersed in the cares of this world, must content themselves on a lower plane.

The feeling of having a share as a citizen in the kingdom of Buddha's children was denied to the laity, much more so even than was such a feeling denied in the old Brahmanical sacrificial faith to the non-Brahman, who, albeit only through the medium of the priest, could draw near to the god equally with the priest himself. The Buddhist believer, who did not feel in himself the power to renounce the world, could console himself with coming ages; he could hope for this, that it might be then vouchsafed to him, as a disciple . .,. of one of the countless Buddhas who shall come after him, to don the garb of a monk, and to taste the bliss of deliverance.[1]

So we find in Buddhist countries to-day the same phenomenon which appears in mediæval history. The monasteries of Europe were no doubt in a sense the forerunners of democracy, inasmuch as prince and peasant might dwell there in equality, but the little democracy itself became a privileged class; as troublesome to kings as the modern nihilist, as the kingly connivance at the murder of Becket shows;

[1] Oldenburg's *Life of Buddha*, p. 387.

and more burdensome to the religious layman than any caste system, as the Protestant Reformation proves.

Undoubtedly the social morality of Buddhism was an advance on that of Brahmanism, but it was as far below the brotherhood of humanity, preached by Jesus, as was the Monkish system of the Middle Ages. In every Buddhist country to-day the monastery is a curse. The traveler who stands amongst the trees of the Japanese monastery and sees the portly abbot, in his yellow robe of silk, seated at ease, while a humble brother adjusts the sandal to his sacred foot; or watches him feed the carp, that flash like gold through the waters of the mimic lake, begins to doubt the reality of his senses. Almost believes that he is in England, that Chaucer is alive, that these men are those whom the poet saw on the way to Canterbury, till he sees them file with downcast eyes and folded hands before the altar bright with candles; then he sees that above the altar there is no image of the gracious Mary, but the sad and noble face of Buddha, and the monotonous chant that surely must be an "Ave," he learns is the Buddhist even-song, "*Om Mani padme om.*"

This is no excrescence that has grown on the stock, as was the monkish system on Christianity; it is a degenerate, but yet a legitimate, fruit of the tree which the Buddha planted.

A second point in which Buddhist morality is said to be equal to that of Christ is in the matter of almsgiving.

It may be said to be almost literally true that a Buddhist "never turns his face from any poor man." A great army of mendicants, male and female, is supported by the offerings of the faithful, most of whom are as poor as the widow woman who relieved the necessities of Elijah.

Certainly we need to pause before boasting of our charities, when we learn that centuries before Christ hospitals were built, and the destitute cared for, wherever the religion of Buddha was preached. But when we come to examine the motive which lay back of this good work, we shall see how far it was removed from the motive urged by Jesus. We have already seen that absolute asceticism was the first step toward the attainment of Nirvâna. The giving up of all worldly possessions was necessary for all who entered on the path of a perfect life, but for those who could not leave all there remained the giving of alms, not, be it remarked, that the necessities of others might be relieved, — that was a mere incident, — but that the hold of the things of this world might be loosened. So that Buddha would never have used the words of the apostle, which lie at the root of all Christian almsgiving: "Whoso hath this world's good and seeth his brother have need, and shutteth up his compassion from him, how dwelleth the love of God in him?" He would rather have said, "Whoso hath this world's good, how can he attain Nirvâna?" Almsgiving, then, was not the sign of a compassion which showed the indwelling love of God; it was the untying of one of the cords that held the soul to life. Christian almsgiving is the sharing of that which is considered a good. Buddhist almsgiving is the getting rid of that which is an evil.

The last point needful to consider in this connection is the forgiveness of injuries. Christ's teaching concerning resentment has always been supposed to be unique. It is true that there have been those who have declared it to be impracticable, but never before have we had reason to suppose that it had been anticipated. But Buddha's charge to his disciples lays as much stress upon the importance of bearing injuries with patience as do Jesus' words to the disciples. Again and again they are told not to resist injuries, not to return insults, but to bear themselves with patience in the midst of a perverse generation.

He who holds back rising anger like a rolling chariot, him I call a real driver; other people are but holding the reins.

Let a man overcome anger by love, let him overcome evil by good; let him overcome the greedy by liberality, the liar by truth!

Beware of bodily anger, and control thy body! Leave the sins of the body, and with thy body practice virtue!

Beware of the anger of the tongue, and control thy tongue! Leave the sins of the tongue, and practice virtue with thy tongue!

Beware of the anger of the mind, and control thy mind! Leave the sins of the mind, and practice virtue with thy mind!

The wise who control their body, who control their

tongue, the wise who control their mind, are indeed well controlled.[1]

There is a beautiful story of a father, who, being murdered by his enemy, with his dying breath said to his son: "My son, look not too far and not too near. For enmity comes not to an end by enmity, my son; by non-enmity, my son, enmity comes to an end."[2] But if we ask the reason that is assigned for a course of action apparently so opposed to the instincts of the human heart, we find that the reason is as far as possible removed from that given by Jesus in counseling the same thing. Jesus said, "All ye are brethren." "Ye must be the children of your father in heaven, for He maketh his sun to rise on the evil and on the good, and sendeth rain on the just and on the unjust." "As your father," Jesus seems to say, — "as your father continues to bless in spite of evil, so do you. Good is more powerful than evil. It will prevail. Ye are all brethren, ye must not return evil with evil, for that is to call forth evil again in him. Ye must quench the fiery darts of his evil spirit in the stream of your love, until, his evil being exhausted, ye save his soul alive." Now whether that be practical or not it is intelligible. We know that what Jesus wished to teach was that every man, who had learned that God was his father, was to be anxious about his brother's soul and not at all anxious about his own dignity, or rights, or peace, if only he might save his brother's soul.

But if we look at the sequel of the Buddhist story

---

[1] *Dhammapada*, chap. xvii.
[2] Oldenburg's *Life of Buddha*, p. 294.

already alluded to we shall learn that nothing was further from the thought of the moralist than this. Passivity was recommended because it was on the whole more profitable than resistance. In the long run the peaceable man would have the best of it; would not beget enemies, but would reap the advantages of peace. So that this doctrine, which at first sight promised to be the anticipation of the Christian doctrine of love, is seen to be a most pusillanimous code, far less likely to lead to moral greatness than the rugged Roman doctrine of virtue or strength. It is not the generous self-surrender of love, but the cool reflection that peace is more profitable than war, which is the mainspring of Buddhist morality.[1]

But there was a deeper reason still, one which lay nearer to the heart of the Buddhist than anything else, and that was the thought that all resistance, all moral excitement, was *agitating*, and any agitation was hurtful. What they were striving to reach was Nirvâna, — the calm that was not blown upon. Whenever they gave way to anger they disturbed the soul's calm. That was why they were not to resist evil. We see, then, that the apostolic injunction to be "angry" yet not sin would have been incomprehensible to the Buddhist. Christ's cleansing of the Temple, his withering denunciation of hypocrisy, which made his disciples think of one eaten up by a zeal for a holy cause, — all that would have seemed to the Buddhist a foolish waste of energy a use-

[1] Oldenburg's *Life of Buddha*, p. 292.

less disturbance of the soul's calm.[1] The sense of duty to a brother's highest good, that can lead the same life to denounce his evil and suffer patiently his resentment, which (together with love to God) lies at the root of Christian morality, would be as incomprehensible to the Buddhist as the pregnant paradox of Jesus, "He that will save his soul shall lose it."

Nothing could have been further from the thought of Jesus than any exhortation to calm. "I am not come to send peace, but a sword;" "I am come to set a man at variance with his father;" "A man's foes shall be they of his own household."

He was continually calling the attention of his disciples to the fact that the following of Him would lead to suffering and disappointment and shame.

Now it was inevitable that this doctrine of non-resistance, because of its disturbing effect on the soul's calm, would lead to the obliteration of all distinction between good and evil. And this we find to be the case. "Those who cause me pain and those who cause me joy, to all I am alike; affection and hatred I know not. In joy and sorrow I remain unmoved, in honor and dishonor; throughout I am alike. That is my equanimity."[2]

It is constantly urged in favor of Buddhism that it was the first religion to inculcate moral exertion as a means of salvation. And certainly in as far as

---

[1] The Neoplatonists were so impressed with the importance of maintaining the soul's calm that they condemned suicide chiefly on that account. See Lecky's *History of European Morals*, vol. ii. p. 43.

[2] Oldenburg's *Life of Buddha*, p. 298.

this served as a substitute for ritualism, it was a great advance on what had gone before. But it will not bear the test of too strict an examination. Buddha himself, and his disciples after him, seem to have been profoundly impressed with the reality of an evil spirit, hostile to the moral improvement of mankind. Yet when we ask how that spirit was to be overcome, we learn from the parable of the tortoise and the jackal. The jackal endeavoring to seize the tortoise he withdrew into his shell, and the jackal having waited long in the hopes of gaining an advantage at length gave over in despair, finding that the tortoise would put forth neither foot nor tail.[1] Moral exertion, then, consisted simply in withdrawing into the citadel of the soul; there the life remained a prisoner to the end. Could anything be further from the Christian counsel, "Resist the devil and he will flee from you"?

This belief in the watchfulness of evil and the susceptibility of human nature to evil begot a timidity of spirit which made the healthy Christian freedom, "to the pure all things are pure," impossible, and so prevented any progress in holiness.

But of course the weakness of the whole moral system lay in the impossibility of prayer. If morality be the "custom'" which has slowly formed as the result of the gradual revelation of God's will, — which is the assumption with which Christian morality begins, — then the thing of most importance is that the "way" for the revelation of that will be kept open by communion between the human and the

[1] Oldenburg's *Life of Buddha*, p. 313.

divine spirit, and that the human spirit by that spiritual exercise be strengthened to receive the same. But Buddhism, starting with the assumption that gods and men were both dependent upon moral exertion, had no place for prayer, consequently moral "exertion" was only self-contemplation, which, so far from being exertion, the effort of the human spirit to commune with the source of light and truth, became, before long, a state of moral and mental abstraction, which led to nothing but self-conceit or spiritual vacuity.

There are some, indeed, who hold that the abandonment of prayer was in itself a distinct moral gain, inasmuch as prayer is essentially selfish. But they have in mind something very different from Christian prayer, the essence of which is unselfishness, which, in the last analysis, resolves itself into a petition that the individual will may not be done. So that, considered simply as a moral exercise, nothing has ever been suggested as so likely to destroy selfishness as Christian prayer.[1]

While, then, we do not admit that the teaching of Buddha on the subject of morals is equal to that of Christ, yet no one can fail to be struck with admiration at two things in Buddhism. The one is the saint, and the other is the missionary. It is easy to call attention to the selfishness, and the ignorance, and the sensuality of Buddhist monasteries, for there

---

[1] "Prayer is just life; inspiration, and respiration, in the kingdom of God: *receiving* and *giving*, the circulation of *Love*." *Letters from a Mystic*, p. 157.

is enough of all; but as in Catholicism there were found a Fra Angelico, a St. Bernard, and these but representatives of a great company of saints known only to God, who, in the midst of the corruption of the Church, were the salt of the earth, so it is in Buddhism.

There are to-day in Japan holy men who sit unmoved amidst all the changing fashions of that volatile people, wrapt in the contemplation of the Unchangeable, so full of dignity, so gentle, so courteous, so peaceful, the fires of passion which once seemed so fierce they might never be quenched are extinguished, and there shines from the life a sort of moon-like radiance that speaks of the day of struggle passed, of the evening of perfect peace. If by their fruits we are to know men, then we may be sure that by such a life has stood one whose name he did not know. If we take note of such a life, we will be sure that it has been with Jesus. No wonder that when such an one dies the monks should feel again something of that thrill which made them tremble when they stood as novices on the threshold of what they thought would be a higher life. We are told they gather about the dying saint, and lay on his heart a coil of spun cotton; and standing round him, and holding each in his hand a thread, to draw some virtue from the holy life they failed to imitate, they say, "I take refuge in Buddha," and the saint replies, "I come to thee, O Lord." "Buddha, save us," cry the brothers, and the flickering breath as it issues from the lips parted in a smile of ecstasy murmurs, "O Essence Divine, with joy, with rapture, I come to lose myself in Thee." [1]

There can be no doubt that such lives have had a profound influence in extending the limits of the kingdom of Buddha. What has been said of the early Christian anchorites applies equally to Buddhism.

The first condition of all really great moral excellence is a spirit of genuine self-sacrifice and self-renunciation, . . . which exercises a most attractive influence upon mankind. Imperfect and distorted as was the ideal of the anchorite, deeply too as it was perverted by the admixture of a spiritual selfishness, still the example of many thousands who, in obedience to what they believed to be right, voluntarily gave up all that men hold dear, cast to the winds every compromise with enjoyment, and made extreme self-abnegation the very principle of their lives, was not wholly lost upon the world.[2]

Of the missionary I may not speak at length, though the subject is full of interest. There have been three missionary religions: Christianity, which ever has and must be such, because it is the religion of the Son of Man; Mahometanism, which proselytes with the sword; and Buddhism, which has spent its force. And yet the annals of the last might be compared for heroism, for zeal, and for results accomplished, to the records of Christian missions. It has been said, The Brahman seeks to save his own soul; the Buddhist seeks to save his own soul by saving another. This is not true of Buddhists

---

[1] This description was given to the author by Mrs. Leonowens, who was present at the death of a Buddhist saint in Siam.

[2] Lecky's *Hist. of European Morals*, vol. ii. p. 156.

in general, yet it is nearly true of the Buddhist missionary, though not as the logical outcome of their system, but rather as the result of the influence of that Spirit which ever breathes on the soul that seeks for good.

And now let us compare Buddhist philosophy with Christian theology, for that must be the test to which we must bring the religion of Jesus. Can it sympathize with mankind? Can it suffer with every part of the great human family in its search for truth? Has it an explanation of that secret which Buddha tried to answer?

We have seen that the starting-point of Buddhist philosophy was sorrow. Buddha called men to him as to one over whom sorrow had no more power, because the sensibilities were deadened. Now Jesus came with the same appreciation of sorrow and began with the invitation, "Come unto me all ye that labor, and are heavy laden, and I will give you rest." Again, He said to his disciples, "In the world ye shall have tribulation, but be of good cheer, I have overcome the world." Not, be it noticed, not by deadening his sensibilities, for we read that so keen were they that "He endured the cross and disregarded the shame, because of the joy that was ever before Him."

And now let us go a step further. The sorrow of life, said Buddha, is caused by the impermanence of life. But Christ felt that too. "Heaven and earth," He said, " shall pass away." He wept when he thought how soon the solid structure of the city He loved should be dissolved. The disciple who came the nearest to his heart wrote words which the Buddhist can appreciate perhaps better than we. "Love not the world, neither the things that are in the world; for all that is in the world, the lust of the eyes, the lust of the flesh, and the pride of life, is not of the Father, but is of the world, and the world passeth away, and the lust thereof;" and these words let us into the heart of the whole question. The religion of Jesus appreciates as profoundly as that of Buddha the sorrow of life; but Christ declares that impermanence is the characteristic only of the "world," that which has no consciousness of the life of the Father in it. Buddhism knows no such distinction. The heroism of the martyr, and the subtlety of the serpent, both are the result of the Skandhas; neither has the life of the Father in it. All shall pass away, said Buddha. But a disciple of Jesus wrote, "Some things shall be removed that those things which cannot be shaken may remain."

Still, it may be said, "After all here are two opinions concerning life: there is something to be said for each; how is one to decide between them?" Let us follow the stream of Buddhism a little nearer to its source. Life, said Buddha, is sorrow. Sorrow is caused by impermanency. Man is carried on like a fluttering leaf, or like a straw that the tide bears on its surface. Here it touches the bank of love, and there it is drifted to the land of sickness and decay. Striving to attach itself to something, it is drifted out to the sea of death, only to float back again between the banks of life. Man is the slave of the circumstances that made him. His personality is the fiction of the Skandhas.

Now what says Christ to this? Says? He says nothing. He stands before us in his majesty, and as we gaze on Him we come to know with a certainty that no logical deduction can attain: That *He* is not the slave of time and tide. He is a *power;* He is not an *effect;* He is a *cause.* Whatever *men* may be, *Jesus* is not a *thing*, He is a person, He is a *king.* We may be the result of the Skandhas, but the perfect man lays his hand on nature's rocks, and they are as wax in his fingers. The voice of the true man calls back the dead. The voice of the true man the waves and winds obey. The true man is nature's master. The perfect man drives back with a word the cloud of sorrow, and the darkened life blooms with beauty as heaven's light rushes in. The perfect man touches the soul all shriveled up with sin, and the life leaps and walks and glorifies God. All this the perfect, the true, the *natural* man does. We have seen but one *natural* man. He does not tell us what he is. He asks us what we think of him, and we try to answer by comparing him with the best of the *unnatural* men, — Elias, the great reformer, Jeremias, the man of sorrow, one of the prophets who foretold a greater. But there is no response. It is only when that which is like a rock within the individual, that which is unshaken by public opinion, answers, "Thou art the Son of the living God," that the Son of Man reveals himself and says, "Thou art blessed." Flesh and blood did not reveal this, no meditation on nature or on man led to this: but my Father in heaven, the source of all life, whom you see in seeing me, hath revealed unto that within you which is partaker of his own life, that the true man is not the result of circumstances, but the son of the living God. That faith is the result of the Incarnation, the manifestation of the Son of *man*. In the power of that man, of that Son, the men and women who knew Jesus "after the flesh," and the innumerable company of those who have known Him in the spirit, rose to believe that they too were persons, — children. In the person of Jesus they saw at once the revelation of the personality of God and the assurance of the personality of man.

The Christian answer to the Buddhist doctrine of the "Skandhas" is the Incarnation of Jesus Christ, the manifestation of one who knew that He "came from God and went to God." "In his light men have seen light." There can be no question that the supposed revival of Buddhism among certain people in our own land is due to the waning belief in the permanence of human personality. It is then of the utmost importance that we should remember that the Gospel assumes the personality of God and of man, and that apart from that assumption the words of Jesus have no meaning. Now Buddhism inherited its skepticism of personality from Brahmanism, but the pantheism of Brahmanism rested on the assumption that the essence of life is *power*. Now nothing can be more certain than that power must return again to its original source. The everlasting division of power is unthinkable. But Jesus' revelation of God is not primarily a Being of power, but of love. But undivided love is as unthinkable as divided power. It is true that

> Love's sum remains what it was before;

but love presupposes an object, and self-consciousness and will. So that if love imparts *itself*, it must impart the essentials of personality. This is not stated in logical sequence in the Gospel, but it is assumed. The essence of personality with Buddha was Kamma, the result of selfishness; the essence of personality with Jesus was love realizing Sonship. "Because we *were* (by creation) sons, God hath sent forth his Spirit in our hearts, whereby we cry Abba, Father," — that is the cry of a latent personality realizing its possibility.

> . . . God's all, man's naught:
> But, also God, whose pleasure brought
> Man into being, stands away
> As it were a handbreadth off, to give
> Room for the newly-made to live,
> And look at Him from a place apart,
> And use his gifts of brain and heart,
> Given indeed but to keep forever.
> Who speaks of man, then, must not sever
> Man's very elements from man,
> Saying "But all is God's," whose plan
> Was to create man and then leave him
> Able, His own word saith, to grieve Him,
> But able to glorify Him too,
> As a mere machine could never do,
> That prayed or praised all unaware
> Of its fitness for aught but praise and prayer,
> Made perfect as a thing of course.
> Man, therefore, stands on his own stock
> Of love and power as a pin-point rock,
> And, looking to God who ordained divorce

> Of the rock from his boundless continent,
> Sees in his power made evident,
> Only excess by a million-fold
> O'er the power God gave man in the mould.

But that personality is progressive. "He came unto his *own;* . . . to as many as received Him, to them gave He power to become (consciously) the sons of God." "God is the only perfect personality."[1] The beauty with which Browning has stated this is equaled by the profound insight which led him to incorporate it in the poem of "Christmas Eve," as the necessary condition of the Incarnation.

That is the real question at issue between not only Buddhism and Christianity, but nearly all Oriental religions and Christianity. It is popularly supposed that man forms his conception of God in accordance with his notion of himself; but I think the religious history of India will teach us that the contrary is true. It was the pantheism of India that made belief in the personality of man impossible. Divinity yawned, as it were, a great gulf at man's feet; into it he must inevitably fall. How was it possible for any individual to stand forth and declare that he alone was a person; not only an effect, but a cause; not merely a creature, but a creator; not merely natural, but also supernatural? Such presumption was impossible save for the man who was conscious of having, before the world was, shared the glory of that unseen, majestic, irresistible, omnipresent power which He could call his Father, the essence of whose being is love and light. Such an one could speak of himself as a Son. Now if in the

---

[1] Lotze, *Philosophy of Religion*, trans. by George T. Ladd.

presence of such an one the Buddhist could come to
feel that he too was partaker of this indestructible
sonship, the very corner-stone of the Buddhist philosophy would be removed, and every noble aspiration and every virtuous deed would find its place
in that building the corner-stone of which is Jesus
Christ.

So much for the relation of Christian theology to
the starting-point of Buddhist philosophy; but can
it go farther and enter into the solemn doctrine of
Kamma?
Of course, if it be once admitted that man is a
person, that death is an incident which the personality survives, Kamma can no longer be regarded
as the survivor of the previous life, — a sort of evil
individuality from which man should seek to escape;
but still that which Kamma represents remains, as
an awful fact, to be accounted for. Pantheism shad-
ing off into agnosticism was the theological basis of
Buddhism, the doctrine of the Skandhas was its philosophical, and Kamma its moral, expression. The
Incarnation we believe to be the answer to the first;
what has the religion of Christ to say to the second?
It cannot be ignored, for the law of Kamma bears
the same relation to ethics that the law of the conservation of physical force does to physics.
We have already described this doctrine at such
length that it will be only necessary to recall its
meaning here. St. Paul's words describe it: "Whatsoever a man soweth, that shall he also reap." Let
us see what that means. Here is a man, we will say,

who has no thought in life save to heap up wealth and gratify his senses. He succeeds; at last he dies. Now what becomes of that force of selfishness which he set in motion? Modern science tells us that by the law of heredity it is transmitted to the man's descendants; it may lie latent for a generation or two, but like a subterranean river it will come to the surface at last. But Buddhism would not rest content with this answer; it would say that is one of the effects, but what have you to say of the man himself? What has been the effect on him? Is he to remain the same forever? What scheme have you for changing him? Or take his case before he dies. Every sin begets the desire to sin. Every good impulse resisted makes a man less able to struggle against temptation. How is a man to escape from the bondage? We see that it is the same problem by which the Jew was perplexed. He had broken the law. How could that violation be atoned for? How could he be free from sin? The Buddhist answer was a perfectly logical one. It was, as we have seen, an exhortation to ascetcism. Suppress every wish and evil wishes will be smothered. Crush every hope and there will be no disappointment. Kill every passion and there will be no lust.

Now the Christian answer was very different. St. Paul, who appreciated as profoundly as any Buddhist the stupendous power of Kamma, wrote, " The law of the spirit of life in Christ Jesus hath made me free from the law of sin and of death." That is a very remarkable expression, " the law of the spirit of life."

There is no escape by violating or disregarding law, only the law of sin and of death is subordinated to the "law of the spirit of life," just as the law of gravitation by which a rock is held fast rooted in the ground is subordinated by the high law of mechanics by which the same rock is lifted up and set for a polished corner of the temple. The Buddhist and Christian doctrine of salvation are as unlike as the different advice that might be given to a man who was about to pass through a plague-stricken city. One would say, Remember that whatever you touch is tainted, therefore eat as little, drink as little, breathe as little as you can; speak to no man, touch no one; the less your contact with life, the less your chance of death. And another would say, Seek to lay hold of the law of life, eat and drink, and fill your lungs with pure air, build up your system, do not think of death; but go your way through the streets of the stricken city, touch all whom you can help, bear yourself like Italy's brave king in cholera-stricken Naples, and the law of the spirit of life will make you free from the law of death.

Now what is the thing that can bring us under the influence of the law of life? For unless we can find that we must admit that the Buddhist is right, that the law of death is inevitable.

The Christian answer is, that the revelation of Jesus Christ has saved great multitudes whom no man can number from the vanity which Buddhism deplores, and from the pessimism which is the Buddhist antidote. How? In this way:—

In seeing the life of Jesus, men have felt the

silent rebuke upon their own low lives. In the admiration which has deepened into love, they have recognized the presence of unsuspected ideals and become conscious of a power to realize them. Forgetful of themselves, they have followed that life along its path of beauty and power, and seen it end in a death which revealed at once not only the vanity but the horror of sin, and yet showed that neither sin nor death can separate God's child from his love and care. Men have come down from Calvary convinced that God is on their side in the battle against sin and sorrow. When they tried to analyze their position in life, they found that the principle of faith by which they identified themselves with the Son of God was the means by which a sense of pardon for the past was produced and an assurance of future salvation. A new principle of life has come into their lives; they have been, as it were, born again. But the Buddhist will say: How about the past? You can't get rid of that; it has produced its effect upon your character. You are still under law. And the Christian will answer: Somehow, since this change has come, the past, which was a burden, is now no burden at all. I suppose my faith in God's power, my faith in God's love, which did not hesitate at the sacrifice of Jesus to bring me to Him, has made me feel that He could take care of the past. But indeed I am not under "law, but under grace." I am like a man who had within him the seeds of consumption, living all uncared for, in a climate that sooner or later would work death; that is to be under "law." I have been led into a balmy atmosphere where day by day a physician tends me; that is to be "under" personal favor or "grace."

So I have learned that health can never be gained by the suppression of disease, but by the gift of the principle of life. I know that I must reap what I have sown, but when I reap I know that the seeds of the grain cannot root themselves in my redeemed nature. I reap in repentance, in humility, in thankfulness, even in joy; for I can in this way enter into the fellowship of my Master's suffering, be made conformable unto his death, and so attain to the resurrection unto a higher life.

However men may formulate the doctrine, the fact has been that, by the influence of the cross of Christ, men have been able to turn their faces away from the Gorgon head of the past, the horror of which has well-nigh petrified the East, and echo St. Paul's shout of joy, "Forgetting those things which are behind, I press toward the mark for the prize of the high calling of God in Christ Jesus." That is the everlasting hope which has manifested itself in individual endeavor and national progress.

If, says the Buddhist, you will only wait, if the soul will, as it were, hold its breath, Kamma will be exhausted. But the Christian says, "'Up, let us be going.'[1] In the cross of Christ I find the assurance of God's pardon for the past and the promise of his favor for the future. If you tell me that law must work itself out to the end, I say that, by the influ-

[1] See Robertson's sermon on the text "Sleep on now and take your rest — Up, let us be going."

ence of Jesus I am being drawn into the natural atmosphere of the soul, and in that atmosphere sin cannot have dominion over me, and sorrow and sighing flee away."

The fact is that Buddhism had not rightly diagnosed the disease of humanity. It is sin, not sorrow, which is a "sore burden too heavy to bear." Sin begins in selfishness and continues from despair. Now the cross of Christ, "constraining" man to love, makes selfishness appear shameful, and the resurrection, opening the pathway to eternal life, slays despair. That is redemption. So that the Christian can say, "It is no longer I that do what I would not, but *sin* which *dwelleth* in me," and in the same breath, "Sin shall not *reign* in my mortal body."

In considering the revelation of the cross of Christ, by which man is redeemed from the power of sin, we find that it not only answers the problem of Kamma, but also throws light on the "Way." The inertness of the divinity of Brahmanism had thrown on man the labor of Sisyphus,— the task of rolling his own soul up the hill of God. The Brahman said the oneness of man and God is dependent upon Kamma, some human "act," *i. e.*, sacrifice. Buddha said: Gods (if there be such) and men are alike the slaves of Kamma, therefore exercise your spiritual nature so as to suppress it. In both religions the inactive East has declared its belief in the efficacy of human effort. And that faith Buddha formulated in the doctrine of the "Way."

To some it may seem as if nothing could be

further from this doctrine than St. Paul's teaching, for he seemed to count all human effort as useless, but that is the result of shallow criticism. St. Paul would have welcomed the moral earnestness of Buddhism; he, too, would have said all men are the slaves of Kamma; he would have agreed with Buddha that this law could never be counteracted by Brahmanical Kamma, or sacrifice; but he would have asserted quite as strongly that it could not be suppressed by self-destruction. What then? Would he have said that man was a passive instrument in this matter of his own fate? Far from it! He would have declared that the law of sin could only be overcome by a most tremendous effort of the human spirit, — by the great Kamma, or act of man's spiritual nature, by which he identifies himself with the conqueror of sin and death, — which St. Paul called, by a power of spiritual insight never equaled, *faith*.[1] By faith Paul meant that absolute trust in God as a Father, by which the prophet had said that the "just," those who have been brought into the right relation to God, live. That trust is the result of the revelation of Jesus Christ: the disciple gains that spirit from his master. The perfectly trustful man is the perfectly "just" man, because the "just," or right relation of the soul to God, is the relation of a child to its father.[2] That trust, St. Paul said, was effected by the cross of Christ. The Brahman was right in declaring the necessity of sacrifice, and

[1] "Religion is never exactly a demonstrable theorem, but the conviction of its truth is a *deed* that is accredited to character." Lotze's *Philosophy of Religion*.
[2] See Erskine's *Spiritual Order*.

the Buddhist in insisting upon moral exertion. Both are justified in Christian faith — the effect of sacrifice and also a spiritual act.

It may be objected that this is not as logical as the Buddhist doctrine. It may be, but it does not follow that it is not true. There is more in man than the logical faculty. This "faith," of which the Scripture speaks, is not, as it is sometimes said, the paralysis of reason. It is the very glorification of reason. It is the powerful exercise of the whole spiritual nature in response to the divine call. When that has been heard, sin is fearful no more, as to the Buddhist, because of its inevitable penalty, but because it is the violation of the perfect law of love.

There remains one more question to consider, and that is the Buddhist doctrine of Nirvâna and the Christian heaven.

To gain *rest;* to find a refuge from which pain can be excluded, a harbor where the soul is no more ruffled by the chilling winds of life : to find a secret chamber and shut to the door, and exclude even self-consciousness, — that is what the tired soul wants. Quiet and rest, and peace and calm. What can be better ? Apparently Christ had nothing better to offer. He came with an invitation to "*rest*," and he departed leaving his "*peace.*"

But Nirvâna and heaven are not the same. Buddha's rest is the relaxation of a soul tired out at the end of life, which sinks exhausted never more to rise. Christ's rest is the unwearied exercise of the highest faculties. It is the rest of the lark, who hangs between heaven and earth intoxicated with the very joy of existence, strong in the consciousness that the eternal winds are uplifting her. Buddha's peace is gained by severing every tie that binds man to his fellows. The Christian peace is found in the perfect accord of kindred souls united in the adoration of the ideal life which at last they see.

Buddha's highest joy was to be found in an absorption which would silence the individual cry. But to the Christian the impatience with this petty individuality gives place to a great hope. *Now* our individuality is like an organ in a damp room. Most of the keys stick, and only here and there a querulous sound is heard. But take the organ into a genial atmosphere, let all the silent notes speak, and then its individuality will be a glorious thing. And the perfect speaking of every human instrument will make the eternal harmony that echoes about the throne of God.

Thus it stands then. Buddha says this individuality is so miserable a thing that no real peace can come till it is destroyed. This individual life, Jesus tells us in the parables of the lost coin, the lost sheep, and the prodigal son, is so precious a thing that it is worth all sacrifice to bring it where it can show its glory. It is only partial now, but hereafter all the unsuspected faculties will spring to life. Every soul shall find itself partaker of all humanity's glories. Each shall be poet and orator, and artist and musician, because each will be a saint, and a saint is a holy man, and a holy man means a *whole* man, and the whole man is he in whom dwells all the fullness of the Godhead bodily. Buddha says to humanity, "You are beaten in the battle of life; you will find peace only when you have reached a place of safety, where no more wounds can come." He appeals to our weakness. Jesus says, "Be of good cheer; I have overcome the world." "In my father's house are many mansions. I go to prepare a place for you." "In that day ye shall know that I am in my father, and ye in me, and I in you." In the consciousness of that power humanity shall wake up after God's likeness and be satisfied with it. No Buddhist anticipates with a thrill the dawning of that day when, in the joyous confusion of that home-coming, the children of God who were scattered abroad find all unexpectedly the gifts that have been prepared for them; when the lame man shall leap as an hart, the ears of the deaf shall be unstopped, the blind shall see. Verily in that day the gospel, the good news, shall be preached to our poor humanity, when we see the things that God has prepared for them who love him. Not an individuality more and more isolated and cramped till it would hide itself for very shame, but an individuality which loses its peculiarities and eccentricities through a development which makes it partaker of all the glory of humanity: that is the gospel of the Christ, and it appeals to the noblest instinct of our nature, an undying hope.

I have endeavored, as far as time would permit, to review the salient points of Buddhism, and compare them with the religion of Jesus. Beginning with the philosophy of Buddhism, we have traced its teachings till they are lost in the clouds of Nirvâna. But it may be said nothing is easier than to refute any religious system by taking a bit here and there, and commenting on it. A religion, like a man, has a right to be justified by faith, and not by works. The true way would be to ask what does a religion seek to do, and so judge it by its spirit.

Now the spirit of Buddhism is pessimism. Its great hope is hopelessness. "Vanity of vanities, all is vanity." That is the Buddhist preaching. On that principle conduct is regulated, and it consists in an effort to lessen the contact with all life, because all life without distinction is vanity. Those who delight to speak of Jesus as the disciple of Gautama point to the same tone in his teaching. "How hardly shall they that have riches enter into the kingdom of heaven!" "Lay not up for yourselves treasure upon earth, where moth and rust doth corrupt, and where thieves break through and steal." But they miss the meaning of Jesus' pessimism. That arises not from the essential vanity of life, but from the vanity of life divorced from God. The interest of a man in the jewel case from which the pearl of great price had been lost — that is pitiful. The child who has lost his father, wandering aimlessly through the splendid palace, seeking to solace himself with toys and baubles — that is pathetic. When the son tried to feed his soul in rioting and drunkenness, he found "the vanity of vanities;" but when he "came to himself," when he came home, the ring and the best robe, the fatted calf, the music and the dancing, were the fit symbols of an eternal joy. Life to the Buddha seemed vain, because there was no purpose back of it. Life seemed vain to Jesus, because he knew the purpose back of it, and saw men warring against it. That thought has been the mainspring of Christian activity. The incarnation of Jesus, the manifestation of the divine in the human, was a revelation of the divine already in the human. It was the holding up of a lamp in a dark room, by which one might see the lost jewels amidst the rubbish of life. "Seek ye first the kingdom of God and his righteousness," said Jesus, "and all these things shall be added to you." Men filled with that spirit have looked on civilization and all its splendor as the outward and visible sign of the inward and spiritual grace of God's favor upon man. Civilization is the gradual adjustment of human life to eternal law.

Against civilization two forces have ever been at work. First, atheism, manifesting itself in materialism, which has always crumbled and fallen as did the splendor of Rome. And secondly, pessimism, which, because it is agnostic, knows nothing of God, is ignorant of the immanent Divine life, loses interest in the symbol that symbolizes nothing, and sinks down to wait for the end. Buddhism, with its pure morality and noble self-denial, ought to have civilized the East. It failed, because like a bridge which men would build across some mighty chasm, there was no hand on the further shore to make fast the cable on which the structure should swing.

So far humanity has seen but one religion which, looking with calm eye on the beauty and majesty of life, has said, "Behold, it is all very good;" "To the pure all things are pure;" and "Love not the world neither the things that are in the world, for the world passeth away, and the lust thereof." Who shall interpret the oracle? It has been interpreted by the Son of Man, who took a little child and set him in the midst, and said, "The kingdom of God is like this; except ye become as little children ye cannot see the kingdom of God." Childlike faith in the father's goodness, childlike love of the brethren, childlike hope which no cloud can obscure, — that is the essence of the kingdom of God. But the kingdoms of the world are parts of the kingdom of God, if that spirit be in them. The only religion which is favorable to human development is the religion of the child Jesus. The power of civilization is not materialism nor pessimism, but the childlike spirit, as the prophet foresaw." The wolf shall dwell with the lamb, and the leopard shall lie down with the kid; and the calf and the young lion and the fatling together; and a *little child* shall lead them." That reign of peace and plenty shall not come with agnosticism, but shall come, the same prophet says, "when the earth shall be full of the knowledge of the Lord as the waters cover the sea."

CHAPTER VII.

HINDUISM.

That Buddhism could not become the popular religion of India, any one familiar with Hindu thought might have prophesied. No "religion" which banished God could long satisfy a people whose whole history had witnessed to the belief that "in Him we live and move and have our being."

Buddhism was a revolt from Brahmanism. The Supreme Being, who dwelt in self-satisfied seclusion, unmoved by the sorrows of men, "careless of mankind," could be nothing less than revolting to the men who had looked on the sorrows of life and felt the bitterness of suffering. Henceforth men would leave the gods in their drowsy contentment and "work out their own salvation." So said Buddha; but the proof that God does not so live is found in the inability of men who had known true thoughts of God to rest satisfied with Buddhism. When and how it was driven from India no one can say. Doubtless it was with war and tumult; but however that may be Buddhism is no longer found as a distinct religious system in India to-day. It still exists in a debased form in Ceylon and in the valleys of Nepaul, but the banks of the Ganges and the plains of the Deccan know it no more.

Brahmanism as it appears after Buddha's reformation is like Catholicism after the Council of Trent; it is the same, and yet it has felt the influence of the times. In this last form, in which it still exists in India, Brahmanism is known as Hinduism.

The origin of Hinduism is shrouded in mystery, but it is probable that it took its rise in that seething time of Indian thought, — the sixth century before our era. It, too, was a protest against Brahmanism, but it differed from the Buddhist movement in this, that while Buddhism began to walk a path which led to atheism, Hinduism set its face from the beginning towards theism. But it was the theism of a philosophic sort, and so in its first form had no attraction for the common people. The power of Buddhism lay in its truthfulness. It did not try to deceive the people. It came at a time when men had drunk deep of the cup of pantheism, and yet cried out for a living God. Then came Buddha and said, There is no living God: the hope of humanity is in itself. The living God has yet to be; you and I are parts of it. Realize the possibility of your nature, and humanity will emerge from the struggle mighty in power.

But the human soul when it becomes conscious of spiritual thirst craves nothing less than the Eternal. To beckon men on with the promise of a God who is yet to be is as vain as to console them with traditions of a God that has been. The first was the error of Buddhism, the second was the weakness of Hinduism, in its first stage, during the lifetime of Buddha or his immediate disciples. We have seen that the Âtman, or one soul of the universe, was often spoken of in Brahmanism as Brahma, or spirit. It was that name on which Hinduism fastened, but instead of using the neuter form the masculine was substituted, and the people were called to the worship of Brahma the Creator.

The call met with but slight response. A few philosophers who had felt the insufficiency of pantheism, but who shrank from the atheism which seemed to be supplanting it, — who perhaps also were disgusted with the "publicans and sinners" with whom Buddha consorted, accepted the new doctrine of the personality of God. Yet, after all, it was but a shadowy personality at best. No one could think of Brahma as one who could be touched with the feeling of our infirmities, — he was a creator, that was all that could be said for him. This was something better no doubt than the inevitable, irresistible law of Kamma, but it was not enough. In their reaction from pantheism the Hindus had fallen short of theism, and so remained in the fatalistic atmosphere of deism. Their God could never be spoken of as "mighty to save." They had, so to speak, waked Brahma from the sleep of ages, but they could not bring him near to man. They had let slip the fundamental truth of Hindu philosophy, that creation is a continuous process, and witnesses to the presence of an immanent, living God. They had lost their hold on that truth, and so could only speak of Brahma as one who had once, by a fiat of his will, created all things out of the Illusion which like a cloud surrounded him.

It was not long before **Brahma** began to sink below the horizon of consciousness, as one who had accomplished his work. That was a dark period in Indian religious life. It seemed as if the only step that could be taken in the direction of theism had failed, and that the last state was destined to be worse than the first. But it was not so. These philosophers had given the clew to the escape from the labyrinth, and the Brahmans were not slow to avail themselves of it.

Hinduism, then, which began as an independent spontaneous movement, contemporaneous with Buddhism, and like it a revolt from Brahmanism, was now taken possession of by the Brahmans, and deliberately used as a means of checking the rising tide of Buddhism. It was to theism that the people were called, and when they responded Buddhism vanished from India like the morning mist, never to return. But it was a theism much more virile than that of which we have just spoken. Atheism was not the only weakness of Buddhism; it was weak because it had broken with the past. The Brahmans, who undertook to revive Brahmanism in the form of Hinduism, knew the value of the continuity of thought; therefore they sought for the deities of the people in the great storehouse of religious thought, the Vedas. If a person was needed to attract the wandering worshipers, the Brahmans determined that he should be the best. We have seen that in the Vedas four gods were originally the heads of the pantheon, — **Agni, Indra, Rudra,** and **Varuna.**

In time Varuna, the god of the cloudless sky, gave place to Sarya, the sun-god, a more active deity. Then Indra began to be spoken of as the same as Rudra, so that there were but three gods left. But these three were but manifestation of the one element of fire : Agni the fire on earth, Indra-Rudra the lightning, and Sarya the sun. In a land where the greatest blessing is rain it is easy to see why Indra-Rudra should soon have come to be spoken of as supreme. It was the old Vedic god Indra-Rudra at once dispelling clouds and bringing rain, blasting with the thunderbolt and blessing with the refreshing shower, that the Brahmans called the people to the worship of, under the name of Shiva, the Auspicious, or the Benefactor, the representative of the creative and destructive forces of nature.

But there was need of more than a name to satisfy people who had known the influence of the searching skepticism of Buddhism. There was need of a philosophy, which would answer the intellectual cravings of the thoughtful. That, too, was found in the past. We have seen that the great monument of the thought of the Brahmanic age was the Maha-Bharata. In its first form it had been no doubt nothing more than a great epic, describing the war between two branches of the great Bharata family. But it had been added to again and again, until it had lost its original character, and was now a great mass of legends, romances, hymns, and philosophical treatises. At what time that part of the Maha-Bharata known as the Bhagavadgita, or Gita, — the song sung by the deity, — was written, we need not here discuss. When it is known that the critics differ to the extent of assigning it to dates eight hundred years apart, it will be seen how impossible it will be for any one to speak with confidence on the subject. The point which interests us, however, in this connection is, that no matter when the Gita was written, it became the philosophical expression of Hinduism, and has so remained to this day. There is a most admirable analysis of this work in Cousin's "History of Modern Philosophy," but the poem itself has been translated into English, so that it may be read of all; therefore it will only be necessary to call attention to one or two points in it which may serve to make clear this part of our subject.

On the morning of the decisive battle between the two rival houses, when the armies are drawn up in hostile array, the heart of Arjuna, fails him, as he sees his kindred whom he is called upon to destroy. In this dilemma he appeals to the god, who incites him to war by pointing out that he cannot kill his relatives, for "there is no existence for that which is unreal: there is no non-existence for that which is real. And the correct conclusion about both is perceived by those who perceive the truth. Know *That* to be indestructible which pervades all this; the destruction of that indestructible Principle none can bring about. These bodies appertaining to the embodied Self, which is eternal, indestructible, and indefinable, are said to be perishable; therefore do engage in battle, O descendant of Bharata! He who thinks It to be the killer, and he who thinks It to be killed, both know nothing. It kills not, is not killed.

... Unborn, everlasting, unchangeable, and primeval, *It* is not killed when the body is killed." [1]

It is easy to see what this mysticism would lead to. It could only end in Antinomianism. The external is nothing. The internal is everything. The letter does not kill; the letter has no existence. Therefore, it is of no consequence what the acts of life are, the only thing to consider is the condition of the spirit! In the Puranas and Tantras, which are the fuller expression of Hindu thought, this theory is carried to its most desperate conclusion. There is something dreadful in this phase of Indian thought. It shrinks from no conclusion. It never seems to occur to an Indian philosopher that a conclusion which contradicts the fundamental instincts of humanity indicates a fallacy. Buddha had glorified knowledge and works, and Hinduism answers, salvation is only by faith and love.

This principle was, however, as much opposed to Brahmanism as to Buddhism. Buddhism was the moral expression of the Brahmanical doctrine of Kamma, or ceremonial. If moral acts were indifferent, much more ceremonial. It was here that Hinduism parted with Brahmanism, and, disregarding the sacredness of the priests, became a democratic movement.

When we consider its treatment of the necessity of " love " as well as " faith " we are brought to more dreadful conclusions. Love requires an object. This was found in Shiva, the Auspicious. He created and

[1] The Bhagavadgita, *Sacred Books of the East*, vol. viii. pp. 44, 45.

be destroyed. The cycle of birth and life, of destruction and recreation, which, as we have seen, was the burden of Buddha's preaching, which he declared was the inevitable law to which all life must submit, which led and could lead only to suffering, the worshipers of Shiva declared was not the effect of an impersonal law, but the work of a personal god. Birth and death, the disintegration and assimilation of matter, in heaven above and the earth beneath and the water under the earth, are all his work, and the result is not sorrow but an eternal joy. He is the Auspicious, he is continually bringing good out of evil. That was a noble faith, more like the rugged theism of Israel than anything we have yet found. But they seemed unable to live by that faith.

The worshipers of Shiva committed the sin of Rehoboam the son of Nebat, and attempted to make sensuous a faith which must ever rest on the contact of the spirit of man with the Eternal. All attempts to realize the generative power of God have ended in the grossest idolatry. We know what came of it in Egypt, in Phœnicia, in Israel. It was the same in India. The temples were soon filled with images of bulls, the fittest emblems of generative power. Finally the bazaars of India were filled with the images of the genital organs as the likeness of their god, and Indian philosophy, which had begun in the purest idealism, ended in the grossest materialism.

It might be possible for a powerful being who brought good out of evil to command the faith, but hardly the love of his creatures, and therefore Shiva was soon spoken of as a being capable of love and as having a consort. No doubt the intention here, as in the worship of the Linga, was pure. The Hindu mind had not forgotten its old dream of Yoga, union with the divine; and there seems to be no doubt that all that was intended by this worship was to typify the union of the soul with God. This thought had been the burden of the prophecy of Hosea, and had been heard again and again in the great and holy words of the prophets of Israel. But it is one thing to speak of the soul as the "Bride of Christ;" to say, "as the bridegroom rejoices over the bride, so the Lord thy God rejoiceth over thee;" and quite another to attempt to represent that union by any visible sign. Shaivism ended, as modern realism must end, in debauchery and shame.

It is true an effort was made to check this descent, and Shiva was, by an act of sublime inconsistency, preached as the ascetic representative of Buddha. But the spirit of sensualism having been evoked in the name of religion could not be so easily laid, and Shaivism descended to its lowest depth in the disciples of "the left hand," as they are called, whose delirious frenzy, the result of the orgies which are to them the highest worship of which man is capable, is such as could not be described in any book.

There are still to be found in India many who have always held to the idealistic interpretation of Shaivism, and who, indeed, utterly repudiate sensualism as in any sense the result of its teachings.

There is one other point in Shaivism to which attention should be called, and that is its doctrine of a future state. The soul that has attained to Yoga will not at death be absorbed into Shiva, but will enjoy the communion with the Auspicious One which has been so inadequately symbolized by the images. It seems at first strange that such a doctrine should have been proclaimed so soon after Buddha's preaching of Nirvâna; but it was more than a revolt from the cold comfort of Buddhism. Buddha, with all his efforts to discourage the "delusion of personality," had done more than perhaps any man in Indian history to manifest the glory and the power of personality; so that it came to pass finally that the way of salvation was felt to lie through faith in the more than human personality of the great teacher. It was here that Shaivism found a point of contact with Buddhism.

"By love and faith," it said, "you can cultivate a personality which, throughout all time, will find a joy in communion with the divine life which the keenest ecstasy of which the body of man is capable will but faintly typify. We have seen how soon the worshipers of Shiva fell from the ideal, and became debased by the adoration of the image; but it would be doing a gross injustice to our brethren of the one great family if we did not endeavor to appreciate as far as possible the religious significance of that from which we at first sight instinctively recoil.

What, then, is the outlook for Shaivism? There can be no doubt that its days are numbered; for while, as we have seen, it was not without good, yet it has failed to answer the needs of the human heart to which it seemed at first to respond.

It began with a message of hope. Men are not

the atoms on which a relentless law grinds without a purpose. Men are the subjects of a king who kills that he may make alive again. But that hope was delusive. It is as fatalistic as Mahometanism, and will succumb to Mahometanism if it be not gathered into a larger truth. And the reason is this: with all its promise of theism, and its revelation of the relation of the soul to the Eternal, Shaivism had not freed itself from the dualism which was always latent in the pantheism of Brahmanism. The union of the god Shiva and his consort is only the old Brahmanic dream of the union of Brahma and Prakiti, the issue of which had been the material universe. Now dualism seems to lead the mind to a satisfying conclusion, because it fastens attention on the opposing *effects* evident in the world — good and evil, while keeping the *cause* out of sight. The doctrine of the unity of God doubtless leads to results which are perplexing, but the history of humanity shows that peace is found in resting upon an inscrutable mystery, rather than upon a solution which seems to be what the human mind requires, but is gained by the violation of a fundamental instinct.

What now, it may be asked, is left for the religion which would convert the Shaivist, but the repudiation of it? Certainly we have so far met with no religion which would be so likely to justify that method; and yet anything which has ever called forth the religious instinct in the heart of man must have that within it on which the religion of Christ can fasten, and rising from which can show the fulfillment of a dream which has apparently violated every religious instinct.

Can the religion of Jesus have anything in common with modern Shaivism, so associated in our minds with Sâti and blood-stained idols and the creaking car of Juggernaut? Yes, for Shaivism, in all its degradation, was a noble effort to find a *via media* between the humanitarianism of Buddha and his inevitable law of decay, and Brahmanic pantheism. The divine essence, said Shaivism, is a person; he has a body like us, and you poor people can come near to him. You have your place in the great religion of which your fathers sung in the Vedic hymns. Think of the old god Indra-Rudra as Shiva your benefactor. This law of decay, to which Buddha says we must submit, is the expression of Shiva's will. He kills and he makes alive. One power is the source of both. Shaivism was the first step back toward a pure theism, and therefore toward Christianity. The Shaivas did for India what Mahomet did for Arabia: taught the people to think of themselves as subjects of a divine king; and incomplete as it may seem to us, it is the beginning of strength, for it calls forth faith in an all-wise, the details of whose government must be wise too. "Let me," cried the great Hebrew king, "let me fall into the hand of God and not into the hand of man;" and the Christian in his hour of greatest agony bows the head and says, "The Lord gave and the Lord hath taken away, blessed be the name of the Lord." That faith strikes its root into Shaivism, but lifts its head above it. Christianity, with its new knowledge of nature, knows that there is no decay save for better growth. Shaivism rests on the faith that good will come out of evil. Its justification is in the beneficence of nature, which kills to make alive. Christianity, with its new knowledge of nature, knows far better than Shaivism that there is no decay save for better growth, but it finds the real justification of its faith in the life of Jesus. His death and coming to life again have done more than reveal a law: they have revealed the divine will toward man. "He that spared not his own Son, but delivered him up for us all, how shall he not with him also freely give us all things?" This man has been declared to be the Son of God with power, by the resurrection from the dead, therefore the disintegration of soul and body in the service of the living God is the pathway to eternal life. That is the message to Shaivism.

Into that second great article of the faith of Shaivism, Christianity can enter with a profound sympathy. It too places faith and love above all things. But it is saved from the degradation which has so often resulted from that faith by the revelation of one in whom the conflict between faith and works is harmonized. Jesus reveals himself as one whose very existence is dependent upon faith in his father. He is the Lamb of God, who waits upon the Shepherd of his soul; but this faith and love are manifesting themselves ceaselessly in doing the will of the Father. That was his "meat and drink." Ever to have missed doing that will which was revealed *by* faith would have been to sever that faith. "Works without faith are dead," but the faith that does not show itself by its works is dead also. That is a truism in the religion of Jesus, but it would be good *news* in India.

HINDUISM.   191

The revolt from Brahmanism to the veneration of Brahma and the worship of Shiva having been successful, it was inevitable that others should follow. So true has this been that Hinduism has been defined as the religion of Sects.[1] There are now ten of these to be found in India, but we shall consider but one more, and that the great rival of Shaivism, called Vaishnuism, or the worship of the god Vishnu.

The name Vishnu also is found in the Vedas, but he plays no such part as the god Shiva, under the form of Indra-Rudra.

Vaishnuism arose like its rival out of the religious conditions produced by Buddhism, and it was an attempt to satisfy the demand which arose, on the death of Buddha, for sympathy and love. Shaivism had attempted to recall the people to theism by presenting a scheme of theology which would satisfy their intellectual needs. It set forth a theology of "faith and love" as opposed to "knowledge and works." The result was the same as followed on the preaching of Brahma as the creator, — it attracted only the philosopher. Shaivism became a popular movement only when it became corrupt. Vaishnuism avoided that mistake, and began, not with theology, but with the preaching of one who was more truly the friend of man than even the loving Buddha, — one who had manifested his love again and again in order to save his people from their sins. There was little enough of this thought in the Vedas, and so the leaders of Vaishnuism went there only for a name. It was the Maha-Bharata to

[1] *Religions of India*, by A. Barth.

which they turned their attention; and under the skillful manipulation to which it was then subjected the great epic became the gospel of Vaishnuism. The god who gave the victory to men, the god who instructed the hero in wisdom, was none other than Vishnu, the Pervader, who, under the form of Krishna, had descended to earth, not for the first time, that good might prevail over evil. But there was another epic on which they laid their hands with a like result. The Ramayana had been originally the story of the abduction of Sita, wife of Rama, by the king of Ceylon. This tradition was to the Indian minstrels what the rape of Helen had been to the poets of Greece. It became a mighty poem, sung at every durbar and recited in every village. On this the worshipers of Vishnu now fastened, and the hero Rama, whose goodness and prowess had been the delight of children for generations, was now used as a mighty engine for the propagation of the new faith. Rama, like Krishna, was a manifestation of the incarnate Vishnu. We may imagine what an effect a story with all the charm of the Iliad might have upon the imagination of a nation when into it was infused the religious power of the Pilgrim's Progress. Yet that was the transformation effected upon the Ramayana. We can easily understand, therefore, how it might come to pass that, as Professor Monier Williams says, "Vaishnuism, notwithstanding the gross polytheistic superstitions and hideous idolatry to which it gives rise, is the only real religion of the Hindu peoples." [1]

[1] *Religious Life and Thought in India.*

One secret of its success no doubt is to be ascribed to its elasticity. And this was due to that fundamental conception of the incarnation which is expressed in the Gita by the Deity. "Whensoever, O descendant of Bharata, piety languishes, and impiety is in the ascendant, I create myself. I am born age after age, for the protection of the good, for the destruction of evil-doers, and the establishment of piety."[1]

We see what an advantage this gave over other systems. Whatever the people loved could be claimed without inconsistency as a manifestation of Vishnu! Is Buddha praised? The accommodating priest declares that he is an incarnation of Vishnu. Is Christ preached? All that is asserted of Him is accepted — only He is an incarnation of Vishnu!

Here, then, are two aspects in which Vaishnuism claimed, and claimed justly, the allegiance of the people. First, there was no good which was not the work of Vishnu. Vaishnuism is as intolerant of a rival as Christianity itself. Secondly, these manifestations of Vishnu are not mere exhibitions of power, they are manifestations of love. They would say with St. John, "For this cause was the Son of God manifested, that he might destroy the works of the devil." But Vaishnuism went a step farther. It could not, after the preaching of Buddha, ignore the past. Rama, Krishna, Buddha, were historical manifestations of Vishnu; there is one more to come at the end of time. But if we look back we shall never find a time when Vishnu was not "making for

[1] *Bhagavadgita*, p. 79.

righteousness." First he was incarnated in a fish; secondly in a tortoise; thirdly in a boar; fourthly in a man-lion; and then in a dwarf.

There is something more here, I think, than simple stretching back by thought into the past. There is a sequence in these manifestations: beginning with the lowest form of sentient life, it mounts to the beast of the field; then to the half man, half brute; then to the manikin; then to the hero; and at last to the saint.[1]

Here I think we may discern a feeling after that great truth of the gradual revelation of the divine life which St. John so emphasizes, and which the writer of the Epistle to the Hebrews announces with so much power. "God having of old time spoken unto the fathers in the prophets, by divers portions, and in divers manners, hath at the end of these days spoken unto us by a Son, — the effulgence of his glory, and the very image of his substance."[2]

Yet with all this promise Vaishnuism has sunk lower than any form of Indian religion. Some of the worshipers of Shiva have retained their purity, but Vaishnuism has gone down as a system. We need not here trace its mournful history, all the more sad because it gave the best promise of redeeming India. It had something worse than the Antinomianism of Shaivism at its heart. It was bad enough to say that the acts of men were indifferent to God as long as there was faith, for faith even in its lowest form implies some sort of spiritual activity; but Vaishnuism lays so much stress on

---

[1] Compare *Indian Wisdom*, p. 336.   [2] Heb. i. 1, R. V.

the last thought of life that an incantation at the end of life will go far to counteract the evil effect of a character which has become ingrained. In the Gita we read, " He who leaves this body and departs from this world remembering me in his last moments comes into my essence." [1] This led also to the belief in the efficacy of rites and ceremonies, pilgrimages and relics. Multitudes may be seen to-day gathered about the well of Vishnu at Benares, in which all sins can be washed away. This belief in the power of a ceremonial absolution has produced the same immoral results in India that the indulgences of Catholicism produced before the Reformation.

Thus Vaishnuism not only proved itself popular with the common people, but it was able to hold its own in controversy by denying the eternity of Shiva. Vishnu, it was said, is the only true God. Shiva has no existence apart from the body in which he now dwells; when that decays Shiva will be no more. Not so Vishnu; he has an existence which is eternal. He is the Pervader. He is independent of all form, and yet has the power and the will to assume many. Thus we see that that doctrine of an incarnation which seemed to be the most inconsistent with the fundamental conception of Indian philosophy has really fallen heir to the powerful doctrine of transmigration, which has underlain every phase of Hindu theology.

[1] *Bhagavadgita*, p. 78. It is true that it is also stated that one will naturally think at the last of what he has habitually pondered on, but there is no intimation that the past will avail if the memory fails.

Has Vaishnuism, it may be asked, then anticipated the doctrine of the incarnation? Williams, in the work before alluded to, tells us that "the Sanskrit language has no exact equivalent for 'incarnation;' the common word is Avatāra, and means 'descent.' Furthermore it must be borne in mind that intervening between the Supreme Being and these Avatāras there must be placed personal deities, such as Brahma, Vishnu, and Shiva, therefore the so-called incarnations ought to be regarded as incarnations *of* incarnations." It is important that this fact should be borne in mind, because no popular objection is more frequently urged against Christian theology than that it has borrowed its fundamental doctrine from India. It was originally urged, I believe by French writers, in the very dawn of the science of comparative religions, but it has reappeared in our own day.

The Indian belief in Avatāra is a belief in a descent, temporary, and to effect a definite object. Again, it is a mere emanation, a belief against which the Christian consciousness has protested from the first formulation of a creed till to-day. That there is a sense in which the Christian incarnation may be spoken of as a "descent," I suppose no one who believes in it at all will deny. St. Paul, in a highly poetical passage in the Epistle to the Philippians, so speaks of it; but throughout the Gospels generally, and above all, in the proem to the Fourth Gospel, the incarnation is spoken of as a revelation or unveiling of the divine reason which had been in the Kosmos and in humanity from the "beginning." In Jesus the scattered rays of the light which lighteth every man that cometh into the world were *concentrated.* In Him the syllables of the Logos were combined to form the word which is the name of God and man, — the divine character in humanity.

Until that fundamental distinction between the Indian Avatāra and the Christian Incarnation is appreciated, I do not believe we can expect any result from Christian missions among the Vaishnavas.

If we are only deists who believe that God once descended into a human form, and that the proof thereof is to be found in the miracles of Jesus, then, I believe that the worshipers of Vishnu will conquer. They too believe in that sort of incarnation, and stand ready to prove it by miracles, compared with which the gracious signs which Jesus gave, if viewed as works of wonder only, are beneath contempt. Did not Krishna lift a whole mountain range on his finger? On what, then, it may be asked, are we to trust as evidences of the Divine origin of Christianity, if not on the physical miracles which served for proof so long? The Christian answer to the human need, — that answering of deep to deep is the best witness to the presence of one who "sitteth above the water floods and remaineth a king forever."

Yet, no one can glance at the teachings of Vaishnuism without feeling that in its doctrine of Avatāras it was prophesying to that incarnation which should be a revelation, not that God had once come to man, but that humanity's name is Emmanuel; that never since man first felt the breath of the Divine life that lifted him above the beasts of the field had

God left him. The message of Christianity to Vaishnuism is not, "You have committed sin in your hero-worship of Rama and Krishna," but, "Your sin began when you left the teachings of the Vedic hymns and the Upanishads, which would have led you to recognize the divinity of man, and saved you from the animal worship which is the shame of India to-day."

It is here that the religion of Christ must find its point of contact with Vaishnuism. Its false conception of the relation of the divine to the human was brought with it out of the degradation into which Brahmanism had sunk at the last. The fundamental idea of the deity was to them power; the fundamental idea of humanity was nonentity; therefore an "incarnation" could be nothing but an Avatāra, a descent of divine power into human weakness. The consequence was that man gained no revelation of the character either of God or of man by any such descent. But the Christian doctrine of the incarnation says, There is a revelation first of human nature, because the light of the world illuminates it; and, secondly, a revelation of the Divine character by convincing men that it is essentially human. Now the reason why neither Greece nor India had any true conception of the character of the Divine was that they had no true conception of what was essentially human. They both identified humanity with what St. Paul calls the "Old Adam," the natural man. The consequence was, that in Greece there was found the apotheosis of vice. There was nothing that men saw in the lives of one another that was not ascribed to the gods. In India there was felt to be no incongruity in the appearance of Vishnu in the vilest woman or the bloodthirstiest man, and that shame was the natural outcome of its faith. For religion must in some way realize its faith in the possibility of the union between God and man. Brahmanism only succeeded in enunciating a theory which destroyed humanity. Buddhism followed with a doctrine which dispensed with God. Vaishnuism preached Avatāras, which had no connection with morality. A god who appears in a hero, an animal, or a saint indifferently, cannot forever command the worship of man. That is the reason of the debaucheries of Vaishnuism. It is to that that modern Vaishnuism has sunk. The hero-worship which began with Krishna and Rama has descended to the worship of brigands; and the worship of Vishnu's consort came, at last, to the honoring of public prostitutes as high-priestesses.

This doctrine of the Avatāra has its reflection in the doctrine of metempsychosis, and, as a saint may have passed into a serpent, the serpent, the ape, and the cow, and every creeping thing, is in turn adored by a people intoxicated with the draught of pantheism, and debauched by the spectacle of unbridled license in a land of lust.

Yet it is here, if anywhere, that the Gospel must speak to the hearts of the people. The incarnation may be preached here as in Greece, not as the descent of divine power, but as the unveiling of the image of God and revealing at once the character of God and man. To the Greek it showed that the belief of mankind that God is human, whatever else

He may be, is true. But it showed that by humanity was meant that sinless Son in whom the Father is well pleased. It must begin at the other end in India; it must reveal the Humanity which is worthy to be called the Son of God. The revelation of the Son of God as the Son of Man was the justification of the faith of the Greek. The revelation of the Son of Man as the Son of God will be the justification of the faith of the Hindu, because the Hindu has never believed that man could have any being apart from God. This must be the point of contact; how much remains then to be done the scope of this book does not permit me to say.

It would be interesting to see how far modern India has been affected by the influx of other ethnic religions, by the invasion of Alexander, the Mongolian inroads, and the conquest of Akbar, but that must be left. The rise of the theistic movement will be spoken of later; it is undoubtedly not the least of the effects produced by the preaching of the gospel of the Son of Man.

It cannot, however, be too often repeated that we must not judge of Indian religious thought by what appears now in the idolatrous worship of modern India. It is the dregs which we see in the cup now, but there has been rich wine there in the days of old; and he who would rouse a people to better things must not begin by scorning their degradation; he must remind them of a great and glorious past, the promise of a nobler future, when they shall see "the fellowship of the mystery which from the beginning of the world hath been hid in God."

CHAPTER VIII.

ZOROASTRIANISM.

THE student of Zoroastrianism is tempted to doubt the existence of any law of spiritual conservation. If there be such a law it must be universal in its application, and yet it would seem to have failed here. Zoroastrianism was undoubtedly once a great moral power in the religious history of the world, but it has been well said that "No other great belief in the world ever left such poor and meagre monuments of its past splendor." Nevertheless, an examination of the history of the Medes and Persians will show conclusively that there is a law that "changeth not," — the law that not an atom of truth is lost in the great march of humanity. A nation or an individual may fail, but the truth which it had in keeping is gathered up by some other nation or individual and made more truly than before the property of humanity.

The present representatives of Zoroastrianism are, as we know, the Parsis, a "feeble folk," scattered from Bombay to Hong Kong; a few of them are still found in Persia, but they are fast dwindling away. So that it may be said that the Parsis are only found as a religious organization in Bombay, whither their fathers fled on the fall of the Persian empire under the mighty blows of the Moslem.

For a long time it was doubtful to what branch of the human family these people belonged. The cast of countenance is not unlike the Semitic type, and on the discovery of the Zend-Avesta by Anquetil-Duperron in 1754, it was believed to be largely composed of Arabic words. But such is not the case. We know now that the Parsis are a part of the great Indo-European, stock, and that their religion sprung from the same root as Vedaism; so that they have a claim to a place among the religions of India.

It is a strange fate which has brought them to India. Their fathers utterly refused to go through the mountain passes into the Punjab; and yet centuries later their children came to India by way of the sea. They fled from Persia to escape the rule of Mahomet, only to see their brethren conquer northern India as the disciples of the Prophet. I cannot think that this is chance. They are evidently a people waiting for something. They still cling to certain ancient ceremonies; they may be seen in the early morning standing on the sea-shore bowing in reverence to greet the rising sun; they still expose their dead on high towers that the earth may not be polluted by the corrupting flesh, but that it may be torn away by the birds of prey; but the great philosophy which lay back of their rites they have forgotten or discarded; they are now a people scrupulously moral and devotedly monotheistic, not ready to die, and yet without vitality to proselyte.

The Bible of the Parsis is popularly known as the Zend-Avesta, but Oriental scholars tell us that we should call it the Avesta, Zend, and Pazend, and that its reputed author should be called Spitama Zarathustra; but we will content ourselves with the popular terms.

If we open the Zend-Avesta at the first Fargard or hymn, we read: —

Ahura-Mazda spake to the holy Zarathustra.

I created, O holy Zarathustra, a place, a creation of delight, but nowhere was created a possibility of approach,

For had I not, O holy Zarathustra, created a place, a creation of delight, where nowhere was created a possibility of approach,

The whole corporeal world would have gone after Airyana-vaêja, *i. e.*, this paradise. . . .

The first and best of regions and places have I created, I who am Ahura-Mazda:

The Airyana-vaêja of the good creation.

The Airva Maineyus, who is full of death, created an opposition to the same:

A great Serpent and Winter, which the Daevas have created.

Ten winter months are there, two summer months.

And these are cold as to the water, cold as to the earth, cold as to the trees.

After this to the middle of the earth, then to the heart of the earth,

Comes the winter; then comes the most evil.[1]

In this hymn Mr. John Fiske [2] finds the record of a tradition of one of the glacial periods which changed Siberia to a land of snow. Dr. James Freeman Clarke [3] also thinks that it is the record

---

[1] F. Spiegel, Eng. trans.
[2] *Excursions of an Evolutionist.*
[3] *Ten Great Religions.*

of the migration of the Aryan family from north to south. Professor Max Müller,[1] however, declares that it is altogether mythical; an imaginary account of an imaginary creation. It would seem, then, as if as yet we could affirm nothing definitely concerning the cradle of the Aryan family. But as we read on in the Zend-Avesta we come to names which we have already met under a slightly different form in the Vedas. The word "Ahura," the name for divinity in the Avesta, we have found as *Asura* in the Vedas. Again, the common name for the gods, "Daevas," is the same in the sacred books of both. Only this is to be noted, the word Asura in the earliest Vedic hymns had a good sense, but in the later hymns the Asuras are the enemies of the gods. But in the Avesta, Ahura is always a title of the highest honor.

The word Daevas or *Devas*, which has descended to our own day as θεύς, Deus, Dieu, Tius in its Teutonic form, whence our Tuesday, Dios in Portuguese, whence the pigeon-English josh-house, this word, on which the religious history of the Aryan peoples might be engraved, came in the Avesta to mean demons or devils. And lastly the chief god of the early Vedic hymns, Indra, figures as one of the chief devils in the Iranian mythology.

One of the few names for the divine which they have in common is Soma or Haoma, for though this is a plant the leaves of which the acolyte pounded in India and Persia alike, and the juice of which the worshipers drank, yet in both mythologies it is also

[1] *Chips from a German Workshop.*

a god. It holds, if possible, a higher place in Zoroastrianism than in Vedaism. It is with the twigs of the haoma (or soma) tree called Barĕçma in the hymns, that prayer and sacrifice are opened.

How are we to account for this likeness between Vedaism and Zoroastrianism? It would seem that originally the Iranian and the Indian branches of the Aryan family had dwelt together as one great division of the human family in its journey towards the ends of the earth.

When it was, no scholar can tell us. As to where it was, there seems to be less doubt.

On the high table-land of Central Asia known to ancient writers as Bactria or Bactriana, named on our latest maps "Independent Turkistan," full of new interest to us as the region in which are Khiva, Bokhara, and Merv, watered by the Oxus and north of the Hindu Kush mountains, the Aryan family seems to have halted in its march.

Could we have looked upon our forefathers as they filled the valleys of the Oxus, we should have seen that conflict between the nomadic and the agricultural people of which, perhaps, the Semitic story of Cain and Abel is a spiritualized reflection. The answer to the prayer of the perplexed Rebecca is the statement of the condition of all the divisions of the human race, " Two nations are within thy womb, and two manner of people shall be separated from thy bowels." "The cunning hunter and the plain man dwelling in tents" were both at that early day in Bactria.

There are two words which serve as torches to

light up the obscurity of this time, they are *kavi* and *kava*. They are from the same root, *kalp*, to celebrate; kavâ is used in the Avesta, as a term of honor, but kavi is a despicable word. This significance is reversed in the Vedas. The explanation given by Haug [1] is this. Kavi was the name of the priests of the united people. They were their leaders. They were prophets as well as priests and kings. To them the people went to inquire the will of the gods. The sacrifice was offered with the intoxicating soma juice, and when Indra was thoroughly inebriated, which happened only when the priests were, one of those marauding expeditions was begun, which ended in the plundering of the more peaceful Iranians who had flocks and herds. No wonder they came to look with horror on the kavi, no wonder Indra seemed a devil. Yet the words had taken too deep a root in their language to be eradicated, and so with a slight change of form the word became the designation of the Iranian kings, doubtless the chief men who first resisted these inroads of their neighbors. They were called kavâ, and so we find the word kavâ in the Vedas as the designation of the enemies of the true faith, while kavi in the Avesta means the worshiper of devils; so we see that the amenities of ecclesiasticism have a strong claim upon the devotee of antiquity.

It was impossible that such a state of things should continue long. The nomadic tribes pushed

---

[1] *Essays on the Sacred Language, etc., of the Parsis*, by Martin Haug. The same thing is described as happening to-day in Tartary, in *Souvenirs d'un Voyage dans la Tartarie*, par l'Abbé Huc.

on through Cashmere or through Afghanistan until they stood at the entrance of the rich plain of India, which lay before them. Into the Punjab the Iranians seem to have come very little, if at all. They preferred a settled life, and began to feed their flocks on the alps of Bactria, and to till the valleys of the Oxus. Soon the schism was complete, and those who would come from the Aryan to the Iranian branch were required to abjure the religion of the Vedas. The form of that abjuration has come down to us. It came to mean in time the renunciation of all evil, like our renunciation of the world, the flesh, and the devil, but in those early days it meant the leaving of one well-known form of worship and throwing in the lot with the schismatics.

"I cease," so said the convert, — "I cease to be a Deva worshiper. I profess to be a worshiper of Ahura-Mazda." "I forsake the Devas, the wicked, bad, wrongful originators of mischief, the most baneful, destructive, and basest of beings."

Thus was made the first recorded religious schism, the first of that great number of protests against wickedness which some may think is sufficiently explained by saying that it was a mere question of occupation; just as some historians think that the Protestant Reformation is explained by saying the monk Luther wanted a wife, or that the American Revolution was caused by the unwillingness of the colonists to pay a slight tax on tea. But the student of history will not rest satisfied with an explanation which confounds the occasion with the cause.

What the cause of this first schism was, what was

the fundamental conception of the divine, which differentiated the Iranian from the Vedic religion, it will be the object of this chapter to trace.

But before we do that it will be well to remember the moral value of a protest. It is often said, and more often repeated, that Protestantism is essentially a negative thing, whereas, in fact, it is of all things the most positive of which the human mind is capable. For what is a protest but the assertion of individuality? The positive action of truth upon the soul of man as opposed to the negative acquiescence in wrong because of lack of spiritual vitality? As well say that the man who lifts a fallen tree out of the path of a band of pilgrims is doing a negative thing because he is resisting the power of gravitation, as to say that the man who, in the power of his individual righteousness, resists evil in opposition to the dead weight of thoughtless acquiescence, is negative in his deed! This, then, is the glory of Zoroastrianism, that it was the first sign of the individual in religion.[1] Now individualism is in spiritual as in material things the first step toward personality. The child must through the sense of pain learn that it differs from the things around it, before it can rise to the full glory of its manhood; and so in religion the soul must recognize the fact that it personally is responsible for wrong, and that its first duty is to separate itself from evil, before it can come to the measure of the fullness of the stature of Christ.

[1] See *Oriental Religions*, — Persia, by Samuel Johnson.

We have seen that it was the failure of the Hindu mind to realize its own personality in the consciousness of a relation to a divine person, which led to the immorality and failure of Indian religious thought. But as personality must begin with individuality, so individuality must begin with the moral apprehension of responsibility, before it can pass into the true personality of the spirit of Sonship. Now the first downward step of Indian theology was taken in Bactria, and the glory of Zoroastrianism began to dawn in that day when the forefathers of Luther, and Latimer, and Knox, and Cromwell, and Wesley refused to believe the orthodoxy of the day, that the divine life could be pleased with the drunken orgies of the kavi.

Undoubtedly individualism has its dangers, one of which is to make any coöperation impossible; but that is what Protestantism seeks, — the uniting of the scattered individuals under the leadership of a strong personality for the furtherance of the truth, which conflict has made more precious than ever. Iranian Protestantism obeyed this law, and found in Zoroaster a leader fitted for the great work of the Iranian branch of the Aryan people.

Strange to say, the life of the reputed author of Zoroastrianism is shrouded in greater mystery than the early history of the religion itself. His very name, which in its Latin form of Zoroaster is so well known to us, has taxed the ingenuity of critical scholars. *Zarathustra* means, according to one commentator, " devoted to agriculture," but another affirms that it means "the golden one," "the color of fire." "He came into the world," says a tradition, "not like all the other sons of men with a cry, but laughing." Biblical commentators, not content with the glory which is in the Bible, but more orthodox than the prophets, and jealous of any truth not recorded in the sacred records of Israel, have found in the life of Zoroaster a Persian version of Shem the son of Noah, of Moses, and of Daniel. Indeed, where so little is known, it is safe to assert almost anything, and lay the burden of proof on the objector.

In such a matter as this we cannot do better than rest upon the opinion of that authority which seems to be the highest. I suppose there is no higher authority than that of Professor Haug, whose essays on the Parsis form a part of Trübner's Oriental Series. It is the opinion of Professor Haug that the word Zarathustra means "most excellent." But we may add that amongst a people avowedly devoted to agriculture it is not strange that he should be called Zarathustra who excelled in the national occupation; and that in a religion the highest rite of which was celebrated with fire, the "fire colored" would be deemed an appropriate name for him whom they venerated as the founder of their cult. But our author declares that this title was originally given to all the priests of the Iranians after their separation from the Indian Aryans, and that the family name of that Zarathustrian who was the father of the faithful was *Spitama*.

He must have lived at a very early date. Certainly as early as Moses, probably before, for while the Bactrian revolt against Vedaism was little more than a protest against certain evils in the established system, this prophet appeared and saved the nation from sinking into nature worship, and called on them to lift up their eyes to the eternal.[1] The earliest of the hymns of the Avesta represent him as talking with God face to face. He stands in Iranian history like Abraham in Semitic, as the "friend of God." In the uncritical period of the science of comparative religions, Zoroaster was supposed to have been the author of the whole of the Zend-Avesta, but scholars now tell us that the hymns which compose this book are of various dates, though the spirit of Zoroaster inspires them all.

The full title of the Zend-Avesta, once the source of inspiration of the whole of the great Iranian people, is "Avesta," and Zend, and Pazend, — that is the Avesta is the ancient text written in Bactrian, and the Zend the commentary on that text written in Pahlavi or ancient Persian, and Pazend a further explanation written in Parsī.

The Avesta and the Zend took their present form, no doubt, amid the horror and confusion which followed the overthrow of the great Sassanian dynasty, when in the midst of the national degradation the priests alone had the wisdom to save the chief treasure of the people, and so justify in the eyes of posterity their national existence.

In trying to reach the *sanctum sanctorum* of Zo-

[1] Bunsen's *God in History*.

roastrianism we will do well to seek an entrance through the ceremonies which are described in the Avesta. Now, if we will recall the contemporaneous rites amongst the Indian Aryans, we shall see that an advance in the spiritual conception of the divine was made by the Iranians. In the Vedas we saw that Agni, the god of fire, was implored to mount on high and bring down the gods to participate in the sacrificial banquet. But here we find no material bond between the worshiper and the divine being.

"Here with Zaŏtra and Barĕçma (*i. e.*, with holy water and the bundle of sacred twigs), I *wish* hither with praise the lords of the heavenly, the lords of the earthly, the lords of the water-animals, the lords of the beings which live under heaven," etc. This formula, so purely spiritual, occurs times without number: "I *wish* hither with praise," or this other, "I invite and announce to the Lords."[1]

So often is this simple ceremony alluded to in the Avesta that one might easily conclude that the consecration of water, the emblem of purity, and the blessing of the twigs, which were the emblem of life, was the only rite recognized in the Avesta. But that was far from being the case. There were more elaborate sacrifices of bread, of flesh, and the haoma juice. These being properly arranged by the priest, the hymn of praise to the immortal gods, whose name was legion, was begun.

Sometimes a victim gayly decked was led to the altar and sacrificed by the attendant priest, but for the most part the sacrifices were bloodless.

[1] Spiegel, *Avesta*.

One of the finest hymns was to Haoma, who is worshiped as a god, while the haoma juice is poured from a silver to a golden cup.

The tenth hymn of the Yaçna begins with an exorcism: —

Away shall then the Daevas hasten which are here; away the male, away the female Daevas.

At the beginning of the morning-dawn I praise thee with words, O Intelligent, whilst I seize the branches.

At the forthcoming of the morning-dawn I praise thee with words, O Intelligent, whilst I slay (the Daevas) with the strength of a man.

I praise the lofty mountains where thou, O Haoma, growest.

Manifestly thou art the seat of purity; increase thou my speech. . . .

Haoma increases when he is praised, therefore is he who praises him the most victorious.

Away vanishes the impurity brought hither, out of such a dwelling, wherever one brings in, wherever one praises, the healing Haoma.

Easy is the knowledge of Haoma.

O Haoma, give me of thy remedies, on account of which thou art (known as) the giver of remedies.

I submit myself to thee as the great dispenser of wisdom.

Praise be to the Haoma, for he makes the soul of the poor in greatness like that of the richest.

Then spake Zarathustra: Praise to the Haoma created by Mazda! Good is Haoma created by Mazda! Praise to the Haoma!

And take this ninth Yaçna: —

Haoma gives to those who as mighty ones make teams to hasten, horses, might, and strength.

Haoma makes manifest to those who are maidens and were long unwedded a spouse, who quickly sues, and is endowed with good understanding.

Haoma is lord of the house, of the clan, of the confederacy, of the region, through his holiness; also lord of wisdom. I invoke thee for strength, for victory, for the body, as very pure nourishment. Come hither with a weapon for the pure to protect the body, O golden Haoma.[1]

Now let us not hastily conclude that this is a vulgar drinking-song sung at a heathen orgy, — far from it. It was a hymn in praise of the Iranian Dionysus, if you will, but he was praised by men who felt that they were wrestling "not with flesh and blood, but against principalities and powers, with spiritual wickedness in high places." They promised to slay the Daevas "with the strength of a *man*," but they knew that that would not suffice, — they needed the strength of a God. Under the influence of the haoma juice they lost the sense of sin, and so concluded that they had become pure. "Thou art manifestly the seat of purity," they sang. Filled with the glory of Haoma they cried, "Thou makest the poorest as the richest." We, who have come to associate Haoma with the spirit of evil, must remember that in its exhilaration the Iranian, like the Greek, found the fittest symbol of the glory of humanity filled with the divine,— and more, identified that which had such power to make the coward brave, the weak strong, the dull wise, and the poor rich, with God who so blesses his children.

Let us turn now to the gods, — see what these

[1] Spiegel, *Avesta*.

people thought of them and what they expected of them.

Amongst a pastoral people we should expect to find pastoral gods, and so it was. One of the chief gods was Mithra. Hé is praised again and again in the hymns. Mithra, the god of vigilance,— with a thousand ears and ten thousand eyes, he watches specially over the wide pastures of the people, doubtless because their chief property was in land, and so arose the idea of honesty. Mithra is the divinity who witnesses contracts, and, finally, it shall be before him that the departed soul shall stand and answer whether he has been faithful on the field of life to his fellow-man.

It is only by remembering this early agricultural and pastoral proclivity that we can understand the frequent hymns to Tistrya — Sirius — the dog-star. The dog is to the Iranian shepherd what the horse is to the Arabian Bedouin. Heavy penalties are decreed for all who injure him, and "Tistrya, the faithful watch-dog of the heavens, is praised as the shining, the majestic one, who goes round about bestowing great joy."

Next to Mithra stands Craosa, the *hearer*. His special watch is just before the dawn, when heaven and earth hold their breath to listen. Before him, too, shall the soul appear. Mithra sees what we have done in the open day, but Craosa hears what has been whispered in the ear.

The tribunal is completed by Rasnu, the inflexible judge. For what they did and said and thought the Iranians were taught they must give an account at the day of judgment.

Time will not permit us to name more of the Iranian gods, nor would it be profitable. The heavens and earth swarm with them. It is an innumerable company; but high above them all sits *Ahura-Mazda*. The eternal, the omniscient God of gods and Lord of lords, the Holy Spirit, the creator of light and goodness, *Ahura-Mazda* — better known to us by the Persian corruption Ormuzd — sits above heaven and earth crowned with light.[1]

The question may be asked, how does all this differ from any of the mythologies? How does it differ from the religion of the Vedas? And the answer is to be found in that fundamental conception of God and of man which lay back of their mythology.

The Iranians seem to have brought with them out of their conflict with the Indian Aryans a most profound veneration for truth and purity. There was, as we have seen, a god who watched over contracts, to whom men must give an account after death. There was no special god of purity, because it was considered the very essence of divinity. It was a characteristic of all the gods. Thus the twelfth Vispered (or hymn) begins: "To Ahura-Mazda announce we this Haoma uplifted. To him the good ruler, the *pure*, to him the ruler over the lords of purity," and again: "The Fravashis (that is the spiritual image of the pure) we praise; Craosa the victorious praise we; the pure man praise we."[2]

The first Yaçna contains sixty-eight verses, each an invitation to a different god to be present at the

[1] *L'Hovique.* [2] Spiegel, *Avesta.*

sacrifice, and the title "Lord of purity," or "the pure," occurs thirty-eight times; and so it is in most of the hymns.

In the seventh Yaçna, which is a long one, nearly every verse begins with the words "with purity I offer" the sacrifice, — and so examples might be multiplied, without end.

No one can read the Zend-Avesta without feeling that the Iranians, more than any people in the world, would have welcomed the beatitude of Jesus as the justification of their whole religious life. "Blessed are the pure in heart, for they shall see God." To live a pure life, then, and a true life, seemed to the Iranian the best thing on earth, — that soul shall pass at death safely over the bridge Chinvah, pass by the fearful dogs that guard it, and stand undismayed before the judges Mithra, Craosa, and Rasnu.

Certainly this is a moral advance from Vedaism. In some respects it is better than Judaism.

But we find a spiritual progress, too, in the Iranian conception of man's relation to the world as compared with Vedaism. The daily conflict between light and darkness the Indian looked on as a spectator, — an interested one, it is true, one who hoped for the triumph of light; but the Iranian felt that he was a partaker in this conflict, that nature's struggle was but an outward and visible sign of a spiritual conflict, in which he must fight for light and truth and purity against spiritual darkness and lies and uncleanness.

"Purity" was to the disciples of Zoroaster what "righteousness" was to the children of Abraham. Righteousness means right relation with Jehovah. Those who would have us believe that it is to be expressed by any such word as "conduct" have tried to understand Judaism without St. Paul's commentary on it. Undoubtedly right "conduct" would be the manifestation of righteousness, but a man might be "righteous" who was guilty of very dreadful lapses in "conduct," as was David, who yet was a man after God's own heart, because not his conduct, but his *motive*, the aim of his life, was right, and that right was the result of his "righteousness;" *i. e.*, his right spiritual relation with God, conceived of not at all as "the Eternal making for righteousness," but as a merciful king living above the sky, with whom David believed that he could talk, and to whom he believed he could sing. "Renew a right spirit within me," said the penitent Psalmist, for righteousness was right spiritual relation to Israel's king and father.

In the same way the "purity" of Zoroastrianism was something more than restraint from impure acts, it was a right relation of man with himself, an internal harmony, something far nobler than the Greek conception of harmony, even the rule of the intellectual and the moral over the material and the sensual. The result of purity, we are told, is the power of seeing God; that internal harmony, which sensualism does more than anything else to destroy, is the means of the revelation of God, because God can only truly be seen by man in himself, and the stained mirror of an impure life can never reflect the beatific vision of the saints. Yet purity alone was not the end of religion, but rather a means to the highest religion; nor is "righteousness" alone enough; righteousness must manifest itself in purity. So we see that Israel had a part of the truth, — the more important, it is true, because the thing of utmost importance is not "conduct," but a right relation with God; but Persia had another part of the truth, and that was the doctrine of purity, without which righteousness would, ere long, become that of the scribes and Pharisees.

Before considering any further the doctrines contained in the Zend-Avesta it would be well for us, at this point, to retrace our steps a little and see how it was that the representatives of righteousness and purity were brought together. It is a marvelous story, — perhaps without its equal in history.

We are all familiar with the story of the Semitic progress in the knowledge of truth, beginning with the Chaldean Sheik Abraham, reaching the zenith of its material grandeur in David, whose dominion was "from sea to sea," and its spiritual splendor in the visions of Isaiah; but the true meaning of the history of the people of Israel did not appear until they were brought under the influence of the Iranians, of whom, perchance, Abraham had known in the days of old.

Imagination must play a large part in filling up the outline drawn by tradition in the history of the Iranian people. The first nation formed from the migrating hordes of Iran, of which we have any sure testimony, is the Medes. There is a tradition that they soon overspread the low lands of Mesopotamia, till then inhabited by the Semites. When they lost their hold upon the south we do not know, but we find them finally established in the northern kingdom of Media. This, then, is the first kingdom in which Zoroastrianism found its home.

It was at this time far simpler than we find it later, as recorded in the Avesta. Whether its dualism had been developed at this time it is impossible to say, but it was latent in it from the beginning. For as a failure to rise to the consciousness of personality leads inevitably to pantheism, so an intense belief in human personality, unmodified by a belief in some "atonement" of the human and the divine, leads to dualism. As soon as man becomes conscious of sin, he becomes aware of his distance from God. Unless he can in some way be assured that, in spite of sin, he is still one with the Divine, he will seek to find some evil principle under whose power he will believe himself to be, and then a divorce between the human and Divine is complete.

There seems to be no reason to think that Zoroastrianism had reached this stage of development at the time of which we now speak; for, had that been the case, we should expect to find greater influence than there is trace of as a result of the inroad of the Scythians, under whose dominion the Medes now fell.

The religion of the Scythians was Magianism, that is, the worship of the material elements of nature, — not as all people have more or less venerated them as the best symbols of almighty power, but as the power itself. The chief of these powers was fire, and to that the highest worship was paid.

This worship of fire was attractive to the Medes in two ways: in the first place they could not imagine a more perfect symbol of irresistible purity, anything that so well expressed their belief that the power of Ahura-Mazda was irresistible. It had also a link with the past. It was the earliest rite of the Aryan people, and had served in the days of old as a bond between the heavens and man, — the only thing man possessed which had power to mount up to the dwelling-place of God.

But it was a descent from the high plane on which Zoroaster had stood, strong in the same faith which had made the Hebrew Sheik the friend of God; and its evil effects were soon seen.

The early Iranians had burned or buried their dead, but now fire was thought to be too pure to touch the corrupting body; the earth also was one of the original elements of nature and might not be defiled; so too was water, and consequently the custom of exposing the dead to the vultures soon became a distinguishing mark of Parsism.[1]

But the Scythian influence did not stop here. In order to keep the fire burning on the mountain-tops, and to decide what in nature was clean and unclean, there was a need of priests, and the Magians stepped in to fill a place which their own doctrine had created, for before this Zoroastrianism had been as free from a hierarchy as the patriarchic congregation of

[1] Drummond's *Origines*, vol. i.

Israel. Such seems to have been the history of Zoroastrianism; the early belief in the Invisible God, who is pure and loves the truth, and with whom men must fight against evil, was overlaid by nature worship, by a sense of the necessity of a priesthood, and confused by subtle distinctions between the clean and the unclean which the trained casuist alone could decide.[1]

But a better time was coming to save them from the corruption which must soon have succeeded this mongrel religion.

A fresh horde of Iranians poured into Media, and under the leadership of Cyaxares threw off the Scythian yoke. Had they thrown off the Scythian influence their history and that of the world might have been changed. But the new king was bent on conquest and turned from truth to power.

We need not follow the history of Media further. The only event that concerns us after this is the fall of Nineveh, hailed with such grim delight by the Prophet Nahum, and all the weary exiles for whom he spoke. His description of the Median assault, and the ignoble crumbling of that great Mammon-worshiping Assyrian empire which had crushed Damascus and Samaria in order to get the trade of Tyre and the commerce of Egypt, is Homeric in its simplicity and passion.[2]

After that Media loses interest for us. It becomes in turn a great conqueror. It invades Lydia, it turns back and enslaves its brethren of the com-

---

[1] Rawlinson's *Five Great Monarchies*.
[2] See Sayce's *Ancient Empires*.

mon Iranian blood. But here it met its death. In 558 B. C., Cyrus, a prince of the royal blood, threw off the Median yoke, and organizing with consummate skill a fresh band of Iranian emigrants overthrew and conquered the Median empire, and took up the work that Media had failed to do, as "Cyrus the Persian."

For twenty years the work of conquest continues, until, in the year 538, he turns his face southward and marches to the siege of Babylon.

The prophecy of Nahum had prepared the inhabitants of Jerusalem to expect deliverance from the Medes, but the fall of Nineveh was the occasion for the rise of the Chaldean empire, far more dangerous to the safety of Jerusalem.

When Jerusalem fell it seemed to the Jews as if God had forgotten them, but the events which followed the first twenty years of their captivity seemed destined to change that fear into certainty.

The Median power which had promised so well did nothing for the captives of Nineveh, and kept on in its triumphant course far north of Babylon. Well for the history of the world it is that it did: for the corrupted Magianism had no treasure for Israel. When, however, Cyrus the Persian arose, the representative of pure Zoroastrianism, he was hailed by a prophet whose words have been incorporated into the prophecy of Isaiah as the "servant of Jehovah." The unnaturalness of Isaiah's prediction of Cyrus's reign, which was once thought to be so essential to the truth of Christianity, has served to obscure the really supernatural character of the faith of the Unknown Prophet, who could welcome this Iranian

conqueror as a man called by God. The twenty
years which passed between the revolt of Cyrus and
the siege of Babylon must have seemed to the people who groaned beneath the burden of the Chaldeans as sure a proof of the failure of prophecy, as did
the railing of Rabshakeh to their fathers in the day
when Isaiah said the city " shall not fall." But again
the prediction of a man of faith, that is of spiritual
insight, was shown to be true. Cyrus came at last
and the city fell, and he who had been hailed as the
servant of Jehovah by the prophet declared that
Jehovah was his God.[1]

The fall of Babylon takes rank in history with the
sack of Rome, and the French Revolution — one of
the three great crises which introduces a new order.

Both Hebrew and Greek tradition unite in ascribing to Cyrus all the virtues which should adorn a
noble prince, so that all that we know of his character tends to justify the faith of the great prophet that
he was the servant of Jehovah.

However the decree recorded in the Bible may
have been colored by Hebrew predilection, there
seems no reason to doubt that in giving permission
to the Jews to return to Jerusalem, Cyrus felt that
he was obeying the will of Him whom the Jews
called Jehovah. It could not have been otherwise
when we remember that the whole strength of the Hebrew people had been tested in the struggle against
the worship of the images of their cruel conquerors,
and that Cyrus was the very embodiment of the

[1] Ezra i. 1–4.

spirit of iconoclasm. It was here that the two religions found a meeting point, and a further acquaintance only served to show the kinship between the spirituality of Zoroastrianism and the true worship of Jehovah. And here we find another example of that which meets the thoughtful student on almost every page of history: the truth that the eternal law is working out the good, though so often it seems as if it must have been deflected by the power of evil. We have already seen that Nahum had hailed the Median triumph as bringing safety to Jerusalem as well as revenge to Samaria, and that it failed to accomplish his hope. Had it done so the Jews would have been brought in contact with a phase of Zoroastrianism so debased by Magian influence that it could only have served to harden them in their belief that God had no care for any people save those in Israel. But when Cyrus absorbed the Median power he restored the pure religion of Zoroaster, and it was to that that Judaism was akin. Even as it was, they came near to destruction by the Magian influence, as we find in the reign of Cambyses, the successor of Cyrus, when, during the Egyptian campaign, the false Smerdis revolted and reëstablished the Magian religion, the influence of which was felt even in Palestine; for it was by his order that the petition of the Samaritans was received, and the work of rebuilding the Temple at Jerusalem was stopped. On the triumph of Darius, the work was renewed, and the Jews were assured of the support of the great king, who revived the worship of the earlier Iranians, and suppressed the foreign rites which had crept in during the Magian power.

These facts it is important to bear in mind, if we would rightly estimate the influence of Persia upon Judæa.

That the Jews actually borrowed from the Persians is not likely. It seems probable that the theory of Kuenen [1] is the correct one: that the Jews, having been absorbed into the great Persian empire, were naturally influenced by the prevailing religious thought of the time, which in its fundamentals was so akin to their own, and consequently had the seeds which had lain latent during the Captivity quickened by the genial warmth of the Persian sympathy.

The first effect of Persian influence is seen in the service of the synagogue. Of course, when the Temple was destroyed the rise of the synagogue was inevitable, if the people were to be kept in remembrance of the great things which God had done for them, and if their children were to be instructed in the law. But we can well believe that at best it must have seemed to the men who wrote the Psalms, so full of devotion to the Temple and its service, but a temporary makeshift. Yet we know that when the opportunity was given to rebuild the Temple but a small part of the people took advantage of the decree. Why was this? Not, I think, because they had lost interest in the religion of their fathers, as is sometimes supposed, for they continued till the fall of the Persian empire to hold the most friendly re-

[1] *History of Israel.*

lations with their kindred in Palestine, and yet to have had no desire to return. Now no one who reads the last chapters of the prophecy of Isaiah can doubt that if the decree of Cyrus had been promulgated by Belshazzar the whole people would have availed themselves of that which, at that time, would have seemed to them most essential for the proper worship of Jehovah. Certainly we do not exercise too great a liberty when we say that this was the result of their contact with a people who had no temple, but believed that God was a spirit and must be worshiped not on the Mount Zion only, but in every place in spirit and in truth. The flight of Jonah from the land of Israel, in the belief that in that way he might escape from the eye of the God of Israel, and the refusal of the captives to return and rebuild the Temple are two great landmarks which show the spiritual progress of the chosen people. So read, the tears of the old men who had seen the first Temple were not called forth alone by the inferiority of the later building, but also by the "New Theology," which was seen to affect even those who had returned to the promised land. The later Temple never became to the Jews what the old Temple had been to Israel. The real worship of the Jews in Palestine, as well as of those of the Dispersion, was the synagogue worship. How essential that was for any real growth in religious thought every student of history knows. It was in the synagogue that Jesus taught and worshiped; it was the Catholicism of the synagogue that Jesus opposed to the sectarianism of Samaria; it was in the synagogue that the gospel was first preached by Paul, and it was after its simple family worship that the service of the earliest Christian churches were modeled. And all this was originally fostered by the people who could not think of God as dwelling in temples made with hands.

Closely connected with the synagogue there began to be felt what we call personal religion, that sense of personal relation to Jehovah which could come only after the idea of a nation in communion with Him, had taken deep root in the national conscience. The latter, we may say, was the fruit of all the experiences of the nation from the day they came out of Egypt till they were carried away captive, after which they were never again an independent people.

But the loss of national independence was more than compensated for by the revelation of personal freedom. The book of Ezekiel is full of this idea of personal responsibility: "The soul that sinneth it shall die." "When the wicked man turneth away from his wickedness he shall save his soul alive." [1] How much such a spirit would be encouraged by contact with the Persians we can guess from a remembrance that Zoroastrianism was essentially a religion of individualism. Righteousness, as we have seen, was the burden of the prophets of Israel; but righteousness had sunk at the time of the Captivity to mean union with a nation chosen by God. Purity was the gospel of Zoroastrianism, but purity is essentially personal.

[1] See Stanley's *Lectures on the Jewish Church*.

Where can we find this more beautifully expressed than in the Khordah-Avesta, a later growth, no doubt, and yet a legitimate one, of the original Zoroastrian thought.

I repent of those sins which burden the conscience; as to see sin and not warn him who does it: to teach evil lying, and inspire doubts of the good: to do harm to any one: to take anything by fraud; to say there is no God; to turn from repentance.

Which I suppose means to turn from the repentant man.

I confess the sins against father, mother, sister, brother, wife, and child.

I confess that that which was the wish of Ormuzd the Creator, and I ought to have thought, I have not thought.

That which was the wish of Ahriman and I ought not to have thought, I have thought.

And yet they too hoped to be justified by faith, for they added to their confessions: —

With all good deeds I am in agreement, and with all evil deeds I am not in agreement. May Ahriman be broken, may Ormuzd increase.[1]

That thought is most strongly emphasized in the prophecy of Malachi. The messenger of the Lord is to sit as a refiner, but who can abide the day of his coming; what individual can stand before him who will try the sons of Levi?

That is the last thought in the Old Testament, a promise that a new day is coming, but a day preceded by the return of a spirit like his who said, "*I*, even I only am left," and "Choose you this

[1] Spiegel, *Avesta*, and *Sacred Books of the East*, vol. iv.

day whom *ye* will serve." With that cry of Elijah so long hushed by centuries of ecclesiasticism, the New Testament opens. "The axe is laid at the foot of the tree. Every tree that bringeth not forth good fruit is to be cast into the fire." Think not to say in such a crisis we are the children of Abraham; the hard heart which yields to God's influence rises up a child of Abraham. Behold the Lamb of God which taketh away the sin of the world is to each individual in the world what the paschal lamb was to each individual in the families of Israel.

This intense individualism was the necessary preparation for the belief in personal immortality which was the glory of Zoroastrianism, and which appears as a leading point in the theology of Israel. No doubt there had gradually been creeping into the minds of the most serious men in Israel a suspicion that death was not the end of the soul's relation to Jehovah; but that was quite a different thing from the strong conviction of the Persian that death is but a crisis in the moral struggle in which the pure in heart shall come off victorious. The suspicion of immortality was deepened into certainty by Israel's contact with Persia. No one can compare the Psalms written before the Captivity, such as the ninetieth, with the book of Daniel, for instance, without being struck with the great progress which has been made in the knowledge of God's will concerning his children. And this hope of immortality also served to quicken their sympathies with surrounding nations. The book of Daniel and the still earlier book of Malachi show this change most clearly. The author of the book of Daniel felt that all the great movements of the human race were tending to establish a kingdom not of Israel, but of humanity, of the Son of Man. Malachi declared that in every nation there were those who were offering incense and a pure offering, and that among the Gentiles the name of Jehovah was being magnified.

It was after the Captivity, too, that there was revived that beautiful belief in the appearance of the angels who accompany Jehovah, which had been a mark of the earliest belief of Israel, but which had gradually disappeared as God was more and more thought of as separate from his people.

So far we find nothing except what was good resulting from the contact of the chosen people with the disciples of Zoroaster. But whether it was that Zoroastrianism fell again under the influence of the Magians, or whether it simply deteriorated as the result of its own prosperity, we cannot tell; certain it is that the later effects of Zoroastrianism upon Israel were most disastrous. That these results were not incorporated into our Bibles is not due to accident; they are a part of the Apocrypha still acknowledged as canonical by the Roman Church, but not by the Protestant Churches, for the Reformers knew that the teachings of the Apocrypha were foreign to the pure religion of Israel. They are akin to that ecclesiasticism which was the result of the contact of the Jews after the close of the canon with the degenerate religion of Persia, after it had ceased to be a power for good in history. It is worth while to examine the dates of Persian history after the return of the Jews from Captivity, for in no other way could we feel so strongly the influence of a guiding hand in the destinies of the people. Babylon was taken by Cyrus in the year 538 B. C. Two years later the Jews began to return to Jerusalem. Darius came to the throne in 522. He openly propagated the religion of Zoroaster, and encouraged the Jews to rebuild the Temple at Jerusalem. The Temple was dedicated in 516. When the Jews departed from Babylon the empire was at the height of its power. Six years later, 510, occurred the expulsion of the Pisistratidæ from Athens, which led to the Persian war. The battle of Marathon was fought in 490, and after that Persia ceased to be a power. Here, then, is a remarkable fact, that the Persian empire was a power while it was giving its treasures to Judæa, but as soon as that was done its usefulness seems to have ceased. To one who believes that the Jewish nation was the divinely-elected medium for the Incarnation, the reason for the Persian existence is seen when, having been led to Babylon, they have poured the pure stream of Aryan theology into the strong current of Hebrew faith, purifying and spiritualizing it.

If, now, we ask what it was that prevented the Aryan religion from supplanting the Semitic, the answer is its *superstition*. St. James, in describing Jehovah as seen in the light of Jesus' life, said, "He is the Father of light, in whom is no shadow." It has been thought that that was the creed of Zoroaster himself. However that may have been, the belief was early held amongst the Iranians that Ahura-Mazda had a shadow, and that this shadow was not the darkness which always lies outside the line of humanity's vision of the divine, but a veritable substance, the great rival of the god of light, to whom they gave the name of " Aüra-Mainyu," or " Ahriman."

As Ormuzd had attendant divinities, so Ahriman was surrounded by an innumerable host of devils, whose delight it was to perplex and hinder the work of goodness. This opinion entered into every department of life. The earth was created, not as the Hebrews believed for the delight of God and man, but only as a means of thwarting the sinister designs of the devil, by localizing, as we should say, the evil. The next step was to divide all things on earth into two classes of clean and unclean. The result of that was to make an endless list of perfectly arbitrary rules for purity. It was the end of freedom. The only science the Persians studied was astronomy. The stars were pure, but the earth was not. The earth being the spot on which the devil is to be vanquished, Ormuzd did not dwell thereon, but apart from the world. His will was known by the revelation which he had made once for all to Zoroaster. The religious consciousness of Zoroaster became, therefore, the standard for all time. The Koran is no more sacred and infallible to the Moslem than the Zend-Avesta was to the Persian, and for the same reason, it was a revelation given once for all by an absent god. He will come again from the distant heaven to judge the world, but he will come as man, — Sosios, the son of Zoroaster, the savior of the world.

Let us sum up now the cardinal points of this creed and compare it with Christianity.

First, then, we find a belief in two rival deities, the conflict between whom led to the creation of this earth as a means of localizing evil.

Secondly, a belief that once in time a revelation was made, but that never since has God spoken to man. The ascription of all the parts of the Zend-Avesta, though written at different times, to Zoroaster only serves to emphasize this belief.

Thirdly, the hope that some day this absent God will return in the form of man as a savior.

And lastly, the conviction that purity is the means by which, in that day, man may be found acceptable.

It was this last point that gave strength to the Iranian religion; for though it made formal distinctions, yet at the same time it was searching, and insisted upon cleanness in the inward thoughts. The fire that burned up all that was foreign to itself was the best symbol of this all-exacting virtue.

But if one wished to find a proof that morality cannot succeed in long floating a system of theology which hinders progress, he has only to study the religion of Zoroaster, which, with the purest morality of any of the old religions, yet gave up its treasures by an irresistible law of attraction to a miserable race of slaves, and crumbled to the dust on the first touch of Greek free thought. And yet this philosophy is the one that is popularly supposed to most resemble Christian theology. That it has had a most powerful influence for evil upon Christianity we are only beginning to understand. We have spoken of the spiritual influence of Persian thought upon the Jews, but that spirit was materialized. It was probably under the influence of later Persian thought that the compilers of Hebrew literature ascribed so many writings of different dates to the old hero-emancipator, Moses, and so taught the people to find the proof of the inspiration of the Pentateuch, not in the quickening of the spiritual life under the influence of a living Spirit, but in the mere historical association with a man to whom they knew God had spoken. The result of this is seen in the cessation of "inspired" writings soon after the return from Babylon.

It was at this time, too, that the doctrine of an evil spirit, the rival of Jehovah, first appears in Hebrew thought. And this belief grew more strong as the thought of an absent God gained ground amongst the people. Then followed the belief in a material resurrection, the conscience of man demanding that by some process this impure matter should be purified. And last of all came the belief that the Messiah would come with a sign from heaven, — a visible witness that the absent God was drawing near to earth.

These were some of the degrading beliefs which the Jews held when their religion had hardened into an ecclesiasticism, under the government of the high priests, far nearer kin to the debased Magianism than to the spiritual worship of the prophets. It was at a time when they had long lost all faith in a living God in the midst of the congregation.

Yet these beliefs which show their influence more or less in the book of Daniel appear still more in the book of Tobit, and became the very life of the Talmud, and were the sum and substance of the orthodox belief at the time of Jesus, the "tradition" which He continually denounced. The washing of the outside of the cup and platter was the parody of the purity of Zoroaster.

The question of Jesus' relation to the popular belief of his day in demons is not one we can enter into here. That there are other beings beside human beings in the kosmos capable of resisting the divine influence is an opinion that no one may presume to dogmatize upon. That they may have an influence upon human life as *diaboli*, the false accusers of man to man, and God to man, has much to commend it. But the opinion which once was taught, but is now falling into well-deserved contempt, is the mediæval notion of a rival to God, whom God has to plan to defeat; a notion that was born of the Manichean speculations of the early Christian centuries, which were themselves the offspring of Persian dualism. But at the idea of rivalry, which is the essence of dualism, the Gospel strikes in the mysterious story of the temptation of Jesus, where we read that the "devil said unto him, All this power will I give thee, and the glory of them, for *that is delivered unto me; and to whomsoever I will, I give it.* . . . And Jesus answered, and said unto him, Get thee behind me Satan."[1] Such an answer would have been impossible for the Persian, because he believed the lie that all power was given to Ahriman, and that to whomsoever he would, he could give it; but Jesus, when brought face to face with that opinion, utterly repudiated it, and said, "Get behind *me*, Satan," the first step towards that sublime statement of humanity's position on earth, afterwards described when He said, "All power is given unto me in heaven and earth."

Look now at that second article of Persian faith, the revelation to Zoroaster and the subsequent silence of the divine voice, an opinion that had such a blighting effect upon Hebrew development, that under its influence the mighty voices of the prophset ceased, a hierarchy took their place to witness to the distance between man and God, the scribes came to expound the sayings of a dead God, and the Pharisees arose to decide where the burning fire of God's righteousness had passed when it had been last seen on earth. Now look at Jesus preaching to the peasants in the synagogue of Nazareth. He is no scribe expounding a dead law; He is a man speaking with that authority which can give an account of itself, to the majesty of which no miracle can add; the authority of one who speaks the things he has heard from God. Under the influence of that life sacred literature revived. Humanity, as represented by those who came nearest to that life, felt itself under an irresistible impulse to cry aloud the glad tidings that God is living

[1] St. Luke iv. 6, 8.

amongst men. The belief has never failed through all these ages that humanity is being led by the Spirit of truth into truth.

The belief that the Messiah would come like the Persian Sosios from heaven, breaking through the visible vault that hid God from man's eyes, — this is the sign that the Jews were always asking for. "Show us a sign from heaven," and that was the sign that Jesus always refused to give. If they could not recognize the divine life when it stood beside them, He would give no sign which would confirm the orthodox heresy that God's coming to man was the return of an absent king. The object of the incarnation was to lead men to see that the divine life which had always been among them was now manifested. That the true meaning of the incarnation was not seen at once, that old prejudices fell off little by little, is only what we should expect. That the full meaning of it is not appreciated yet, that every advance in the history of man has only served to throw new light upon it, will surprise no one who believes the birth of Jesus Christ to have been the supreme act of history, the explanation of the past and the prophecy of the future.

Now one of the first effects of that notion of an absent God which sprang up in the Christian Church as the result of a revival of a debased form of Hebraism, and the influence of the dregs of Zoroastrianism which still lingered in Asia Minor, was seen in the prevalence of the belief in the superiority of the ascetic life.[1] God had made the world,

[1] See *Histoire du Gnosticism*, par M. Jacques Matter.

and left it, and now the devil ruled, therefore the less we had to do with life the better. It was dualism working itself out into practice that produced that monstrosity of asceticism which Theodore Parker said was the daughter of atheism and sensualism.

It may seem as if the subject of this chapter had been forgotten, which is the relation of Zoroastrianism to Christianity; but indeed just as one who wished to study the true meaning of Wycliffe's common-sense religion would have to go to Bohemia to see how it burned, like great lumps of sea coal, under the influence of the southern character, or as one who would judge of the best fruits of the political French writings in the eighteenth century would have to leave the Bastile and the Place de la Concorde and stand on Bunker Hill or in Independence Hall, so he who would see the outcome of Iranian theology must leave the Euphrates and stand beside the Jordan and the Tiber.

We have seen how much Jewish thought was indebted to Iranian spirituality, and how the continuance of the Hebrew religion was the justification of that spiritual faith, but it remained for Christianity to justify the essential element of Zoroastrianism. The necessity of purity for a knowledge of God had been from the beginning the conservative force of the religion of Zoroaster. And this Christ justified, not by simply adopting it after the method of eclecticism, but by deepening its meaning and showing upon what it is dependent. "Blessed are the pure in heart," said Jesus, "for they shall see God."

If these words had come down to us as the saying of an unknown teacher, we might well have concluded that he had felt the influence of the Iranian religion; but they are the words of one whose life is a witness that a purity which is not a formal ceremony, but a living principle of the heart, is *dependent* upon the constant seeing of God. The life of Jesus is the counterpart to the Beatitude, Blessed are the pure in heart, and they that see God are pure. One of the disciples felt this when he wrote that the effect of the full vision of God would be similitude, "we shall be like him, for we shall see him as he is;" and another formulated the very Augsburg Confession of spiritual freedom when he wrote, freeing the Christian Church forever from arbitrary distinctions, "to the pure all things are pure."

But as this purity was not to be a matter merely of ceremonial observance, neither was it to be produced by the observance of any rules. It was to be the effect of the consciousness of an indwelling Spirit of holiness, the highest gift of God.

Zoroastrianism had begun with some such thought. As long as God was thought of as communing with man, so long had purity been a state of the spirit. When God was thought of as absent, purity clung to "observances." The whole history of religion shows that the two go together: the worship of an absent God must be the "tithing of mint, anise, and cummin;" the service of the immanent God is "mercy, judgment, and truth." By the gift of the Spirit, Jesus insured the purity of his Church.

Out of that faith in the power of purity, that of the possibility of individually knowing God, sprung a faith in the everlasting existence of the life that had talked with God. Crudely as that belief may have expressed itself, grossly as it may have become materialized, it may be questioned whether the resurrection of Jesus could have found acceptance, had not Zoroastrianism prepared a *nidus* for that belief. But the resurrection of Jesus, whatever may have been its physical aspects, was invariably spoken of by its witnesses as the fulfillment of the law of Christ's being. "It was not possible that he should be holden of death." It was declared both by Peter and Paul in their first recorded sermons that Jesus was the Christ, the Anointed Man, of whom it had been said of old that He could not see corruption. Or, as it is more strongly put by St. Paul elsewhere, He was declared to be the Son of God "with power, according to the spirit of holiness, by the resurrection from the dead;" in other words, it was in accordance with the spirit of holiness (which includes Hebrew "righteousness" and Persian "purity") that Jesus rose from the dead. That which the Psalmist had declared to be the law for the Son of David, the disciples of Zoroaster had taught was the reward of each man's struggle against evil, and that faith the Son of *Man* justified. Justified it as He did the Hebrew faith in righteousness, by showing that it was a far nobler and better thing than any reanimation of the flesh; even a life which exceeds in glory and power the present life more than mature manhood surpasses trembling infancy. Of the Son of

Man even it was said, in reference to his Resurrection, This day have I begotten thee; as if the life that the earth had seen was nothing as compared with the life that burst upon Him who had been dead and was alive again.

The part played by Zoroastrianism in preparing the world for the resurrection must not be overlooked, for it is its greatest glory. It was the first religious system to feel the power of personality, and proclaim that it was a spark of the divine flame which should neither be "blown out," nor absorbed by the consuming fire.

Zoroastrianism has been called Oriental Puritanism. I would prefer to call it the John Baptist of the Ethnic prophets. In some respects it was the nearest to Christianity, and in others it was the farthest removed. It was destined to decrease while that must increase. Christianity could not deliver it from the prison-house of superstition; but when it sends asking, "Art thou that which should come, or do we look for another," the answer is, "For this cause was the Son of God manifested, that he might destroy the works of the devil," and "Blessed are the pure in heart, for they shall see God." It says this, not as a rival system of philosophy, but as the witness to a life which revealed the power of humanity to conquer sin, and the reality of humanity's dream of "seeing the King in his beauty," in the "power of an endless life."

CHAPTER IX.

"THE PERVERSION OF THE GOSPEL."

As we look back over the path which we have marked, we see that the early Aryan religions were feeling after an answer to great questions, to which the Christian Church, influenced by the spirit of Christ, believed that they were answering in that summary of the Christian faith called the Apostles' Creed. To the first article of that creed Vedaism brought its problem of creation, saying, We know of the divine as omnipresent and kind. But Jesus knew the divine as the immanent creative power, — no blind force, but an everlasting Father upholding all things by the power of his will.

In Brahmanism we found that the divine was conceived of less as a principle of matter, and more and more as a spiritual image, immanent in man and recognizable by man's spirit, and that true bliss consisted in the union of the divine image in man with the indestructible essence of life. But we saw, also, that this divine essence was impassive, — having no power to effect this union. To the aspiration of Brahmanism the doctrine of the Holy Spirit, quickening the latent image, inspiring with the hope of reaching the measure of the stature of Him who is the perfect image, leading to a union which is the reconciliation of a son and a father, comes as a gospel.

We have seen how Buddha, looking on the sorrow of life, declared that there could be no escape save by the cessation of desire. That the fiction of personality was at the root of all delusion, and that if men would but free themselves from delusion by detaching themselves from life they should enter a perfect peace where they would desire nothing. We saw how Christ came with as profound an appreciation of sorrow as Buddha, but that He declared it was inherent not in *life*, but in the "world," — that existence in which there is no consciousness of the Father. He said that He was come that men might have "abundant life," and that the pathway to life lay, not through the deadening of sensibility, but through the death of selfishness. And yet, with all his hatred of selfishness, He so magnified the glory of personality that He opened a heaven of endless progress in the knowledge and love of God, which, He declared, was eternal life.

We saw, also, in the inevitable revolt from the nihilism of Buddhism, the rise of Hindu theism, with its Shiva, the God of life and death, and Vishnu, the preserver. Into sympathy with that more profound religion we saw that the Church could enter, because it has the Gospel of the Word made flesh, which justified humanity's faith in its own divinity, and revealed God as a character essentially Christian, — like Shiva, the giver of life and death; like Vishnu, the preserver. And this gospel is not a story of some *Avatāra*, a sudden and temporary descent into a human form to effect a specific purpose, but the history of the Incarnation, which has revealed the mysterious power which redeems human nature from death and sin.

Lastly, we retraced our steps to the starting-point of Aryan history, and followed the Iranian revolt against Aryanism to the time when it yielded up its treasures of spirituality and purity to Judaism. But we saw the weakness of Zoroastrianism, too,—the arbitrary distinctions between right and wrong, its absent god, its completed revelation, its hostile power of evil. We found that Christ set his seal to its inherent truth, but repudiated the parasitic growths which had well-nigh strangled it. And that these might never hinder the truth again He called together a Church, an assemblage of the faithful, who would "judge all things" in the consciousness of the power of the indwelling Spirit of truth, and in hope of eternal life through Him who had been dead and was alive again.

Compare, then, the results of Vedaism with the Christian faith in the Fatherhood of God, Brahmanic aspiration with the Gospel of the Holy Spirit, Buddhist despair with the story of the Cross and Resurrection, Hinduism with its "feeling after" Him who is not far from any of us with the doctrine of the Incarnation, Zoroastrianism with its purity so inadequate with the belief in the Communion of saints, and then ask how it came to pass that a peasant of Galilee inspired men with a faith which reveals Him as the desire of all nations.

The anomaly of that character cannot be too often insisted upon in questions of this sort, and yet that character itself cannot be rightly appreciated if it be considered only in its manifestation in the three years of Jesus' ministry; we must look to his body the Church if we would see what Jesus' life is. For in some way it came to pass that the Church was founded. A company of men and women were called together. Some overwhelming emotion awaked in them the consciousness that they were nearer to Jesus and saw more clearly the Father than in the days when Jesus was visible to the eye. No doubt they were unable to explain this until Paul appeared, and declared that it was because the same Spirit which had sanctified Jesus was an inherent part of human nature. This thought was carried on by John, and the Christ-Spirit was declared to be the portion not only of the Christian, but "the light that lighteth every man that cometh into the world." So that the difference between the Christian and the non-Christian was not like the difference between the Buddhist or the Zoroastrian and the Brahman, — the difference which exists between the members of various sects; it was simply the difference between one who knew what relation humanity bore to God and one who did not know it. We hear a good deal about the corruption of the simplicity of the Gospel by the speculations of philosophy, but it was not until the Gospel had been "corrupted" by St. Paul that the Church began to understand that Jesus had not died and risen in order to form a sect in the midst of Judaism, but the Catholic Church. And that was absolutely a new thought in the history of mankind. None of the religions which we have considered every dreamed of a church, much less of a Catholic Church. Buddhism came the nearest to it, but we have seen that it soon was compelled to draw a line between the secular and the consecrated life, and establish religious orders to realize what it was admitted man was unequal to. And even had that not followed, Buddhism at the best could never have attracted the West; for the characteristic of the West is activity, which is the deadly sin of Buddhism. If it be answered that Christ violated instincts of humanity as deep as that for activity, — as in his teaching concerning revenge, — the answer is that He never violated an instinct of humanity.

No doubt it seems as if He did, but if by an instinct of humanity is meant such an ingrained sentiment — no matter what its origin — as is capable of progress, then with revenge as with all other things Jesus was "set for the falling" before there came the "rising of Israel." Revenge in its brutal form is the desire to inflict suffering because of suffering caused, but it is only transfigured revenge which cries, "Father, forgive them!" There is an instinct in the human heart which demands that evil shall not triumph over good. The man who has lost that has lost an essential part of his humanity. The simplest way of preventing the triumph of evil is the infliction of some punishment which will equal that inflicted, and so prevent the preponderance of evil! But Christ revealed a better way when He said, "Pray for them that despitefully use you and persecute you." And under the influence of that spirit revenge, which was the protest against the triumph of evil, gave place to the enthusiasm for conversion, which is the demand for the coming of the kingdom of God.

The Catholic Church, then, is nothing less than the calling of humanity to realize its humanity in the Spirit of Jesus. And that it cannot be too often repeated is a new thought, a veritable gospel to mankind.

But the Church could never have been built up had it not been that individuals had already, in part at least, realized that life which the Church was to declare to be the true life of humanity. The record of those Christians before Christ, found in the Jewish Scriptures as in the literature of no other people, the Christian Church took with it, and said that that which had been realized in narrow bounds and in partial ways by a people who felt the presence of God must be realized more perfectly by men and women who had been brought by other ways to the knowledge of the truth.

For a long time that was the only Bible the Church had: when the Apostle went to the synagogue he reasoned out of that; when he went to those to whom it was unknown he spoke of God's message which comes in the falling rain and the warming sun, or he turned to the poetry with which they were familiar, and led them through that to God. But this new experience of the indwelling Spirit was producing a literature which was to be more precious to the world than the Prophecies and Psalms. The epistles to the churches soon were found to be of larger application than had been supposed. The Philippians were addressed as men, and in this gospel to men there was a lesson for every man. Then as the eye-witnesses passed away it was felt that the tradition of Jesus' life must be gathered before it was too late, and in the Gospels there was embodied the portrait of Him who walked among men and made them know that they had seen the image of God. Thus our Bible grew, and it became, together with the Church, the great witness to the truth. The one witnessed to the immanence of God in society, that gathering together of individuals in a common faith which we call the Church; and the other witnessed to the immanence of God in the unpremeditated aggregation of men in the nation, — God in history; while the life of Jesus, recorded or unrecorded, witnessed to the immanence of God in the individual because in humanity. That is the threefold witness which is to convince the world.

And now the question which may well be asked, and to which it is hoped this book will give some sort of an answer, is this: If Christianity be the satisfaction of the great human needs and wants as expressed in the religions of the world, why has it failed to conquer the world? It has not conquered it. Europe and America are nominally Christian; but Central Asia is Mahometan, while from the Ganges eastward Buddhism is the religion which has absorbed all the rest. Yet for fifteen hundred years Christianity has been helped by the wealth, the material power, and the intellectual ability of the world. Its Founder gave it a world-wide commission. It began with a missionary spirit that seemed destined to sweep the world with its enthusiasm, but it did almost nothing in the East. Its triumphs were chiefly in the West, and now its force seems spent; it is not converting the heathen, and it is with difficulty that it holds its own against the advancing tide of intelligence in Europe and America. Why is this?

It ought not by any means to be admitted that all that is implied in these objections is true; on the contrary, it might be possible to show that the missionary spirit of the last twenty-five years has done an apostolic work, but it is best to place before ourselves as clearly as possible what it is that is being said against the religion of Christ, and recognize that it has power, because we ourselves feel that there is truth in the objection that we are not doing what we ought to be doing. But the important question is not, Are we doing what we might do if we entered more fully into the spirit of Jesus? but, Has that spirit so spent its force that it is not possible that intelligent men should be inspired by it to-day as they were eighteen hundred years ago?

To answer all that such a question implies would necessitate the writing of the history of the Church, but these few facts should be remembered in any such discussion.

In the first place, the Gospel was, as Paul said, a "treasure in earthen vessels," and the first mistake of the Church was when the Roman Empire was allowed to gild those vessels with flattery. In that day the glory of serving gave place to that of ruling.

But the Church had hardly seated herself in her new empire, had hardly time to show whether the Christian spirit could predominate over the traditions of the past, before the storm of the barbarian incursion fell upon her. No greater proof of her vitality could be educed from history than the fact that when the storm had subsided the Church alone, amid the wreck of principalities and powers, lifted up her head. But the sight that met her gaze might well have appalled the stoutest heart; the civilization of centuries destroyed, and half-naked savages, drunk with their titanic orgies, the masters of the world. That Christianity should have survived such a day of judgment, that the Bishop of Rome and his brave clergy could ever have had the faith to begin the rebuilding of the world, is sufficient proof of the vitality of the faith of Christ in the year 452 A. D.

The conversion of the barbarians to Christianity was a wonderful, but to us a most unsatisfactory piece of work. Of course, if we were shut up in a block-house on the frontier with a drunken savage, we would try to tame him before we began to convert him. Now the truth seems to be that the Church was so glad to get the barbarians tamed that she compromised there and called them converted, consecrating all their ceremonies which were not immoral, and alas! absorbing many of their superstitions. The consequence was that mediæval Christianity was composed of three elements; the simplicity of the gospel of Christ, the imperial policy of Rome, and the barbarian superstitions. The Reformation was the great national protest against the imperial policy of Rome, and a religious protest against the barbarian superstitions. The full meaning of the political revolution we know now means that which the authors of it never dreamed it could mean,—democracy. The goal of the religious movement, we are only now beginning to see, is the liberty of the sons of God.

So then when any one brings it as an objection against Christianity that it has spent its force, the proof being that the early missionary triumphs of the Church were greater than our own, it must be remembered that the Church had had no time to free herself from the seductions of the state alliance before the incursion of the barbarians occurred; and that from that day till the Reformation mediæval Christendom was what the author of the "Continuity of Christian Thought" calls a "parenthesis in the larger record of the life of Christendom."[1]

It may be asked why more has not been done to convert the world since the Reformation. The answer is that far more has been done than ever before. More Christians have been made in the past one hundred years than in any six hundred before. Perhaps this cannot be said of the number of *converts*, but the question cannot be decided by statistics; for no one who considers what the life of Jesus was supposes that the converts made by the Jesuits in Canada or by Xavier in Japan are to be counted among the triumphs of the cross! But the real reason why more has not been done since

[1] *The Continuity of Christian Thought*, by Alex. V. G. Allen, D. D.

the Reformation is that the Reformation is not yet finished. Up to this time its work has been largely negative. Its positive work has yet to be done, or rather completed. For of course nothing could be more positive than the English Revolution, the American Revolution, and even the French Revolution, all of them the outcome of the Reformation.

Nothing could be more positive, also, than the scientific effects of the Reformation; but when I speak of its negative results I mean theologically. The reason why its results have been so positively good in politics and science is that they were born as the result of that great labor, but theology had been held in bondage, and has not yet been set free. The Reformation will not have finished its work until the spirit of dogmatism has been put down. And when I say dogmatism I do not mean agreement in the acceptance of certain facts,— nor even in opinion about those facts; in that sense dogmatism is an essential element in human society; but when I speak of dogmatism, I mean the spirit that insists upon intellectual agreement in regard to details which in the nature of the case we must be ignorant of, as, for instance, the exact condition of the dead; which discourages historical criticism because there is supposed to be a fixed tradition concerning the canon of Scripture which may not be violated; which decides that scientific discoveries must be held back until the scribes have examined the text of Scripture to see whether the admission of truth is "safe;" which, in fine, would turn the Church into a club, into which no one may be admitted whose intellectual condition is not entirely satisfactory to every member, and which makes the acceptance of metaphysical speculations upon inscrutable mysteries the test of fellowship with Him who said, "Come unto me, all ye that labor and are heavy laden," and "If any man is coming toward me I will in nowise turn him back." That spirit has been the shadow of Protestantism, and prevented the power of the great religious revival of the sixteenth century from being felt. Is that spirit on the increase or not? It is on the decrease. This new and fashionable spirit of agnosticism has certainly done this good. It has made men ashamed of their dogmatism. The theologians have been like two heated disputants, and agnosticism, instead of taking sides, has simply said, Neither of you know anything about the matter. It has stopped the dispute; it has set men to thinking as to the grounds of religious certitude. It has led multitudes to feel that the truth of any spiritual announcement is to be proved, not by an external miracle, nor by an unbroken tradition, but by the immediate response of the human soul to that announcement. As Maurice has well said, "Conscience is not the measure of truth, but it is its *test*."

No doubt agnosticism itself may become dogmatic. It has done so. It has asserted with the old *odium theologicum* that God is unknown and unknowable. But we need not be troubled by its dogmatism; we may be sure that it has become dogmatic, because it has no new message. For I suppose it is always true that men become dogmatic when they are conscious that they have nothing new to say, and so fall

"THE PERVERSION OF THE GOSPEL." 255

to reiterating the old statements until they gain a certain sanctity which they never had in the early days when they were only the preliminaries of something better. No one who can read the signs of the times at all can fail to see that the Christian spirit, so far from being hurt by the dissolution of dogmatism, has really begun to feel the pulse of a new life. It is the old fond delusion, that a captive bird would die if set free in the forest, that leads men to think that Christian liberty needs the cage of dogmatism. History shows that it does not need it. When the Reformation has done its work it will be free.

But dogmatism is only the intellectual symptom of a disease of which institutionalism is the ecclesiastical. The bane of the Roman Church has been institutionalism, with all its materialistic philosophy of a spiritual effect to be produced by a material act. That heresy has prevented the heroism of the Jesuits from bearing its legitimate fruit. Xavier and Loyola and other Catholic missionaries devoted themselves to enrolling their converts in a visible army, trusting to the organization to effect a change of heart and life. The bane of Catholic missions, rooted as they are in institutionalism, has been politics. Owing to the heroic labors of Xavier, Japan was at one time nominally almost a Christian country, but the wicked attempt of the Jesuits to place a so-called Christian prince on the throne of his father, the heathen Mikado, led to a revolution which apparently ended in the martyrdom of thousands at the rock of Pappenburg in the harbor of Nagasaki. But that was not the end; a prejudice was produced against the religion of Christ which is only beginning to give way to-day. Indeed, it is said that in the interior of Japan crosses are still set up on the Tokaido, and the little children are taught to spit at them as expressive of the utter detestation by the people of the religion that they warmed in their bosom, and like an adder stung them. Institutionalism has been the bane of the Jesuits. But the day of institutionalism is waning. The American Revolution was the dawning of a new day, when the instrument of the divine power was no longer to be sought in an ancient institution, but in the federation of individual men inspired with the hope of a great purpose. That dawn was obscured by the clouds of the French Revolution; it may be retarded by the sycophancy of Teutonic socialism or the madness of Russian nihilism; but it is sure to come, and those who live to see that day will find that the religion of Christ has again the opportunity which it once had, and which the institutionalism of Rome and the dogmatism of Geneva have prevented it having since to influence individual men and women conscious of the true glory of humanity in the life of the Son of Man.

But dogmatism and institutionalism are themselves symptoms of a deeper evil, and that is sectarianism. Now it was against sectarianism that the Reformation protested! That great truth has been obscured by historians, because they were confused themselves about the matter. For what is the essence of sectarianism? Is it not that spirit which denies that salvation or truth or virtue can be had out of a certain *section* of the Church? Well, where did that spirit ever manifest itself as in that section of the Church which was ruled by the Bishop of Rome? It was against that sectarianism that the Reformation protested.

In France that protest took the scientific form of reconstructing what was supposed to be the original organization of the Church, and became Presbyterian. In Germany the national mysticism manifested itself in the preaching faith, spiritual insight, as the *summum bonum*. In England it followed the course of the national proclivity, and expressed itself in a conservative government under law, violating as little as possible the tradition of the past. So far there were, if we may so speak, more sects and less sectarianism; that is, the Christian Church had been marked out in certain well-defined lines, but there was no attempt to insist that any one of these was the norm for all Christendom. It was the Roman Church which was full of the old spirit, and insisted on its sect dogmas and its sect organization. Had the unity which at first prevailed between the Lutheran, Genevan, and Anglican churches continued, the world would have been nearer the kingdom of God than it now is. But the demon of sectarianism is not so easily exorcised. First there came the sectarian dogmatism of Luther, and then the institutional sectarianism of Calvin, and then the institutional sectarianism of Archbishop Laud. Then came the second wave of the Reformation, the great Puritan revolt. But sectarianism was not yet dead, and division has followed division, until it has come to be believed that the object of the Reformation was sectarianism, and the results must be either the dissolution of the Christian Church, or a return to some previous form of belief and organization which all will accept. It seems strange that this plan should commend itself to thoughtful people. And indeed it does not; that is to say, no thoughtful man thinks well of the plan unless it be stated as the return to his own denomination. It seems stranger still that it is not recognized that any part of the church which calls itself the Catholic Church, as distinguished from other parts of it, is only placing itself in the unenviable position of Bunyan's "brisk young lad coming out of the country of Conceit whose name was Ignorance."

Yet in spite of all this no one can be found to defend sectarianism! All are agreed that unity is the one thing needful, as indeed it is, but no one need dream that unity is to be obtained otherwise than as our fathers thought. God had inspired them to obtain it by protest against all that makes against it. For unity is not uniformity either of doctrine or of discipline. We have seen that, and the Church scarcely survived it. Differences of opinion are essential to active spiritual life, and active spiritual life is essential to morals. Those who ask that men should lay aside their theological differences are asking they know not what, — a return to that day when theology, the knowledge of God, was the treasure of a *class;* when that day comes there will be a loss of interest in God, a loss of faith in God's revelation of his character to men, and, consequently, the immorality which has always succeeded. Equally vain is the dream of one organization. Were it obtained to-day it would be overthrown to-morrow. What then is the outlook? Further divisions? It may be. For no unity can be obtained until it is clearly seen what is to unite. That only can unite which is an integral part of the body. Certainly the sects are not that, — neither Roman, Anglican, Lutheran, nor Genevan. They are all the work of men. The Church is the body of Christ, and the *members of that body are individuals*. Every *individual* in whom the Spirit of Christ dwells is a *member* of his flesh and of his bones. If that be true, all this talk about the sect to which he belongs not being a part of Christ's body is apart from the question. It ought not to be said that any organization is a member of Christ's body. St. Paul told the Corinthians that they were members "in particular." If then the individual is a "member," he, with all others who are so inspired, constitute the Church of the living God, and they are one in Him. That body, as St. Paul says, cannot be divided. That is the unity of the spirit, the bond of peace. Any other union would be a bond of discord. What then, it may be said, is the value of this unity, if it cannot make itself effective? But it can. In the first place, many of the sects will die the day this unity is recognized, because at best they have had but a galvanic sort of life, the result of the friction produced by some "establishment," and will be re-absorbed into some stronger form of life. But of those which remain there is no reason why there should not be effective unity. If only each would forego its claim to Catholicity. Calvinism and Lutheranism, Anglicanism and Romanism, are but the expression of great human needs which always have existed and always will exist. Let them exist. Give up all attempts to proselytize from one part of the Church to another, and let Christians as Christians unite for the conversion of the world. Let a baptized man be counted a Christian, and then let him worship God and express his belief in his Saviour in that way in which God has spoken to him.

But it will be said we need a common creed to express our belief! Well, we have it. Every man who calls himself a Christian believes in the Lord Jesus Christ. But there, it will be said, is the difficulty. One thinks of him as "God over all blessed forever," and another as only the best of men. How can those two commune together? Why not? Are we sure that Matthew and Paul and John could have drawn up a creed that would have satisfied each in all respects? Are we sure that each disciple meant the same thing when he assented to Peter's confession, "Thou art the Son of the living God"?

And if not, do we believe in truth, and think that it will not make itself known to men through men? Are we afraid that the Unitarian will convert the Orthodox, or do we believe that Unitarianism is an anomaly, and that it has always appeared in certain conditions, and will reappear again in like conditions? I have placed in the forefront that question which of all others stirs, and rightly, the hearts of Christian people. But if that can be seen to be solvable, then no other ought to trouble us. We ought to be able to eat the bread and drink the cup with any disciple in the presence of Him who is our Saviour and our King. No more reason is there that we should refuse so to do than that we should refuse to look on the rising sun with one to whom it spoke only indefinitely of promise and hope, while to us it was the veritable witness that God was living and lighting his people.

That this is the unity which St. Paul praised when he wrote, "In him is neither barbarian, Scythian, bond, nor free, but Christ is all and in all," seems too plain to need argument; but if not, indeed there is no argument that will convince any man, because it goes down to the eternal question, What think ye of Christ? If Christ accepts a man as a follower, can those who have Christ's spirit refuse his company, or make conditions which he cannot accept without the violation of that conscience which has led him to Christ? Of course there will always be "groups" of disciples, but this "grouping" is not schism; that is the deadly sin of resisting the Spirit of Christ which alone makes us members of his body.

The effect of such a unity as that of which I speak would be seen at once in missions. It would be recognized that there are in heathendom potential Methodists, Anglicans, and Calvinists, and that when they become Christian they will inevitably follow their predispositions. Therefore we should be content to carry them the gospel in its simplicity, and encourage them to organize themselve on the lines of that division of the Catholic Church which seems best to answer the needs of their nature. That simplicity was the characteristic of the Apostles' method seems clear enough. They told the story of Jesus' life, and when men felt themselves drawn to that life they said, "It is the revelation of the character of God," and into the name and character of God they baptized every man who said, "I believe in Jesus Christ." The secret of their success lay in their simplicity.

How they would have dealt with differences among their converts we may learn from the way in which they dealt with them among themselves. Peter and Paul and James differed in their understanding of the meaning and scope of the Gospel as much as Cardinal Manning, Henry Ward Beecher, and Bishop Huntington; therefore they agreed to differ. Paul went to the Gentiles and Peter to the Jews, while James remained in Jerusalem; the only thing they had in common was their love for the Master of whom they thought so differently. That was the second secret of their work: they perceived that God had different ways of revealing Himself to different men, and no one of them claimed to know all and be all.[1]

---

[1] Into the question of the sectarianism of the disciples of Peter and James and Paul the scope of this book does not permit us to enter; doubtless it was far greater than is generally supposed. That Paul

That is the spirit of the Catholic Church, and when that spirit again prevails the Catholic Church which has survived Romanism and Anglicanism and Calvinism, which contains them all and is none of them, — when that returns, then the world will believe that the Father sent the Son to be its Saviour. Dogmatism will give place to the love of truth, and ecclesiasticism to free organization for the expression of a new energy.

There is one more characteristic of the Apostolic method which must be revived before the great work of converting the world can succeed. St. Paul, who is the ideal missionary, laid it down as a fundamental principle that to the Jew a man must become as a Jew, to them that are without law as without law, to the weak as weak, all things to all men, that he might by any means save some. Which means that by the power of that enthusiasm for humanity, which was the effect of the gift of the Spirit of Jesus, he threw himself into sympathy with the religious wants and experiences of the people to whom he preached. It is necessary to take but one of the many examples of this adaptation which meet us on every page in the history of his missionary journeys.

In that fragment which has come down to us of his great sermon on Mars Hill, Paul says not one word about Hebrew law and prophets. It begins

was persistently followed by the Jews of Asia Minor, and to some extent by "certain from James," "false brethren," is clear enough. How far the overthrow of Pauline Christianity prepared the way for the collapse of the Syrian and Asian Church, on the Mahometan inroad, is a question yet to be investigated.

with the announcement of the revelation of an unknown God to the agnostic Athenians; it goes on to speak of the relation of this God to temples, to that nation of artists; it declares the brotherhood of mankind to that democratic state; it announces the immanence of God to the fellow-citizens of Socrates; it declares the divine sonship of humanity to those lovers of beauty; it announces a judgment by a Divine Man to those idealizers of humanity; and a resurrection from the dead to those Greeks who loved life well and hated "dark death." And this is declared to be the fulfillment not of Hebrew prophecy, but of Greek poetry; he does not quote Isaiah, as when he spoke in the synagogues, but an ode of Cleanthes. That was the method of Paul, that was the secret of his success in Europe, and the truth of this will be seen if we turn from the Apostolic successes to their failures.

The Apostles were successful all around the Mediterranean Sea, but there are traditions which we may not ignore that they went to the far East, and even to the land of the Scythians, yet no monument of their work is found. Why that should be has never been explained. I believe it was because they found themselves among a people so far removed from Hebrew, Greek, and Roman thought that they were unable to fulfill the first requirement of missionary success as laid down by St. Paul. They could not place themselves in sympathetic accord with the people among whom they were. Surely their labors were not in vain. Their example has been a stimulus in all ages; but it has been left for our own day to enter into such political and commercial relations with the East as to enable us, if we wish so to do, to preach the Gospel in India, China, and Japan as Paul preached it in Europe.

The Apostles were successful in their efforts to convert the Jews who still held to the faith of Abraham, by answering their demand for *righteousness*. They were successful in preaching to those Greeks who had not sunk into utter sensuality, by answering their idealism. They converted those Romans who were not utterly brutalized, by answering their efforts for an universal brotherhood.

But when they passed beyond the influence of Roman, Greek, and Hebrew thought, the advance was checked. Why was this? Because they knew God in part and man in part, but not yet *nature;* consequently when they found themselves in the East they came in contact with pantheism, which underlies all Oriental thought; with that they could not *sympathize*, and therefore had to fall back into that region in which the chief interest centred in humanity. St. Paul's experience, when he was forbidden by the Spirit to go into Asia, was an epitome of the Spirit's government of the whole Church. It was led westward, God intending that from the West the light should turn back again toward the East.

I do not say that no mission work has been done in the East: far from it; but no *nations* have been converted as in the West. Heretofore we have had to convert *individuals* by separating them from the national life, and, consequently, Oriental converts have always been more or less unsatisfactory. They have rarely been the best type of their people, for in the best type the national idea would be strongly manifested; but we have been able, so far, to do little with the national, or perhaps it would be better to say the race, idea. If we are ever to convert a nation or people, it must be by converting individuals on the national or race line.[1]

[1] The success of the Nestorians in the East is very suggestive. Nestorius was too much influenced by the dualistic pantheism of Gnosticism, but the East recognized in his disciples men who felt the majesty of the Divine too profoundly to use the doubtful expression "Mother of God," and who recognized the immanence of God so keenly that they shrunk from saying that God was "born." Nestorian missions might give the clew to the Church by which the Incarnation might be preached in the East. For a statement of Nestorius' position, see Milman's *Latin Christianity*, vol. i. book ii. chapter iii.

CHAPTER X.

THE FUTURE OF CHRIST'S RELIGION.

WE have seen, in the last chapter, how the Gospel was perverted; but for that the Church would long ago have outgrown the necessary limitations of the Apostolic age and converted the world. The question which we need to ask before this work is brought to a close is, Are we in any better condition to do that than the Apostles Thomas and Bartholomew? We have no new gospel. We have the same message that they had. We must hesitate before we say we know the Master better than they. What, then, is our advantage? I think we know the East better. We are better able than they to "become to the Orientals as an Oriental."

And that will be more evident if we consider the drift of Western thought.

The great study to-day in Europe and America is Natural Science. What has it taught us? I do not mean what has it taught us about the weight of the moon and the distance of the sun, for, as Matthew Arnold says, people care very little about that; but the eager world has been crowding around the scientist while he keeps his eye to the telescope or the microscope, and crying, What do you find about God? No doubt there have been many to say,

We have found that there is no God, and the godless have cried, "Then let us eat and drink for to-morrow we die." But the true scientists have grown more profoundly reverent, more deeply impressed with the presence of mystery back of all phenomena, year after year. No rolling worlds have been discovered in this crowded space which are not subject to law; no minutest particle of dust has the microscope revealed that does not receive and transmit force. Now law has no meaning except as expressing *orderly arrangement*, and force has no meaning save as the expression of the result of the exercise of *will*. Science, then, has banished forever the atheistic notion of *dead* matter. There is no such thing. We know, says science, no matter that does not reveal force and law. Back of all phenomena is mystery. No doubt science has been dogmatic, — a necessary condition of partial knowledge. No doubt the religion of positivism has declared that God is unknown and unknowable; but we do not need, because of dogmatism, to reject the truth that commends itself to our reason. Whatever science may say when it puts on the robes of religion, as long as it remains science it declares the immanence in matter of the unconscious God as law and force. If science could discover the Christian God in nature the Gospel story would be overturned, for that begins with the statement that the divine reason was in the Kosmos, and that the Kosmos was made by it, and the Kosmos was not conscious of it.

If we turn to the East we find that the books which are most popular to-day are the writings of the positivists, — not, I am sure, because of their dogmatism, but because they recognize that which the East has always declared: that God is nowhere if He is not in nature. One of the best tracts that could be distributed in the East would be Wordsworth's poetry, which is filled with the thought of Christian pantheism, which is the doctrine of the immanence of God. I say, then, that just in proportion as we can enter into sympathy with the Oriental adoration of nature will we be able to preach the gospel of the Logos, who was manifested not only in nature but also in man.

What, then, is the outlook for a return to St. Paul's sympathy with the religious aspiration of the Gentiles? The new science of comparative religions is making ignorance of the faith of mankind impossible. The gradual effect of that knowledge is instructive. Father Bury, a Portuguese missionary, expressed the feelings of religious people, when the spiritual treasures of the East were first opened, by saying of the Buddhist ritual in China, "There is not a piece of dress, not a sacerdotal function, not a ceremony of the court of Rome, which the *devil* has not copied in this country." [1]

When that simple theory was abandoned it was asserted that the Buddhists had copied from the Nestorian missionaries, — and if rites, why not opinions?

The dogma that truth could come to man only through the teachings of the Church drove men to

[1] Quoted in *Ten Great Religions*.

strange expedients. But if any one would appreciate the change that has come to the Christian temper in the last century, let him compare these two quotations, the first from the Preface to "Paley's Evidences," and the second from the Preface to the "Sacred Books of the East," by F. Max Müller: —

I desire, moreover (says the archdeacon), that in judging of Christianity it may be remembered that the question lies between this religion and none; for if the Christian religion be not credible, no one with whom we have to do will support the pretensions of any other.

I most heartily agree with that statement, but I would be sorry to think it true if by Christianity we are to understand Paley's notion of it; but the real animus is to be found in the determination not even to consider any other religion.

Now listen to this: —

To watch, in "The Sacred Books of the East," the dawn of the religious consciousness of man, must always remain one of the most inspiring and hallowing sights in the whole history of the world: and he whose heart cannot quiver with the first quivering rays of human thought and human faith is unfit for it. . . . What we want here, as everywhere else, is the truth and the whole truth: and if the whole truth must be told, it is that, however radiant the dawn of religious thought, it is not without its dark clouds, its chilling colds, its noxious vapors. Whoever does not know these, or would hide them from his own sight and from the sight of others, does not know and can never understand the real toil and travail of the human heart in its first religious aspirations; and not knowing its toil and travail, can never know the intensity of its triumphs and its joys.

Paley would prove the brightness of Christianity by comparing it with the darkness of heathenism; Max Müller would let the glory of Christ's religion be judged in the light of the Gentiles.

One other cause of the poor success of Protestant missions may be named. Buddhist and Mahometan missionaries have this advantage over Christians, that it is an easy thing to practice what they preach, to conform to some outward sign. Jesuit missionaries have the same advantage over Protestants, that they can point to faithful imitation of ecclesiastical rites as a proof of conversion. But the Protestant goes with the message, " The kingdom of God is not meat and drink, but love, joy, and peace;" and when he is asked for examples of Christians, he has to acknowledge with shame that drunken sailors, selfish merchants, and godless travelers answer to that name. I suppose the one thing a missionary would most dread for his convert would be that he should visit a Christian land. Such an one would not see the patient, heroic, noble lives that are following Christ; he would see the dens of iniquity winked at by the law, the degradation of the Christian poor, and the selfishness of the rich. He would see great armies of men kept from peaceful labor that they may defend their homes from Christian neighbors, and Christian fleets built to ravage heathen lands.

Had Christian people as nations sought the kingdom of God and his righteousness, the meanness of capital and the grasping selfishness of labor would be as impossible as slavery. We have failed to realize the brotherhood of humanity, and that is why we hear in our own land the frantic shriek of the anarchist, and see the destruction of life and property in Europe. Men talk about that thing being suppressed by force; they might as well talk of driving back malaria into the swamp. The land must be drained or the evil will continue, and we may believe that Nihilism is our day of judgment which no generation shall escape. We may believe that in the clouds thereof men shall see the appearing of the Son of Man, and that a further step will be taken toward the realization of the brotherhood of mankind.

These are some of the forces for the coming of the kingdom of God which are working while men sleep, — Agnosticism and Nihilism, Democracy and the study of the science of comparative religions. There are others which we have not yet spoken of, because they are not evidently working against certain well-ascertained hindrances to the spread of the kingdom, but they are none the less working for it.

What, then, is the outlook? I believe that the outlook for rational, that is spiritual, that is Christian, religion was never so bright as now. Those who live in fear that history may repeat itself, and that savage hordes may again devastate civilized lands, have not learned the lesson of history. That is no more likely to happen than the evolution of a new type of life, which scientists tell us is finished.

What we must look for is a mental and moral modification of the highest type — man. If that be true, then man is but in his moral and intellectual infancy, and Christ has come not at the end of history, with but little time left for humanity to realize his life, but in the very dawn of history, as soon as the infant man could hear the divine voice. We need expect no more overturnings of society by barbarians. We know the world; we know what to expect. Macaulay's vision of the New Zealander on London Bridge is vain. The world is free to begin its development as far as external dangers are concerned. Its real dangers are internal, and menace the religious life. But already we may see the signs of better things. The theological and ecclesiastical discussions which have broken out afresh after slumbering so long must drive men a little nearer to the realization of the unity of the Spirit as they see the futility of any unity of compromise.

In attempting to answer the various objections which come to our ears, I would not leave the impression that the Christian Church needs apology after apology. When it is asked why more has not been done, — and that question must be asked by the faithful disciple, — it is well if we can find how it has come to pass that the work has been hindered, and better still if we can see the signs of better times, through a return to the Apostolic spirit. Both of these I have tried to do, because they are essential to an understanding of the future of Christ's religion. If there are any who think that the reasons assigned are not the true ones, such would do well to study carefully the history of missions, and see whether the work has not deepened and broadened as the better spirit, the manifestations of which have been great in the last hundred years, has influenced churches and individuals.

Should this spirit prevail still more we should see an enthusiasm for missions, such as has never been seen in our day; for the Church would feel that in her power to "fulfill" she was destined to great triumphs in awaking the heathen to an appreciation of their own treasures, in the faith that they would not rest satisfied in them, but through them pass to the discipleship of Him who has the words of eternal life.

And yet I would not mean to imply that all our dangers are behind. They are not. There is great danger lest knowledge be divorced from faith. We are living in one of the great epochs of history. Our children's children will look back to this day as our fathers looked back to the day of Copernicus. What Copernicus did for astronomy, Darwin has done for natural history. Life can never be the same again. The churches may reject the new knowledge, and grow hard and narrow. Ecclesiasticism may refuse to obey the law of "Divine Providence," and insist upon its own willfulness. Disgusted by sectarianism, thoughtful men may grow indifferent to the truth, and thus hinder the progress of the Church. But the most dreadful danger is that atheism within the Church which denies we are under the guidance of the Spirit of truth, which we hear the sound of, but cannot tell whence it comes or whither it goes, only we believe that it is the Spirit of the Father and of the Son. These are some of the dangers and some of the forces working for the future. And when we speak of the forces which are working in behalf of the kingdom, we are only speaking of certain manifestations of the Spirit's presence in politics, in philosophy, and in society; but we have no name by which we can describe that mysterious awakening of men's souls in our day to a deeper apprehension of the work of Jesus, which is more truly the characteristic of this age than the facility to invent or the enthusiam to discover the secrets of nature.

And now turn from the problem of enlightening the theology of heathendom to this still more perplexing question of the elevation of its morality.

It has often been thought that this is a hopeless task, that it is useless to attempt to place before men any particular statement of moral worth, because there can be no such statement. It is a matter of climate, or of food, or political institution, or national temperament. That which is considered right among one people is thought to be wrong among their neighbors. Each nation develops a morality which is proved by experience to be the most expedient for its peculiar condition. Penalties are enacted to insure its enforcement, and public opinion " cements a cake of custom " which the individual finds it hard to break. To have a uniform morality necessitates a uniform climate, and the same food. But the answer to all that is, that nations whose climate has remained the same, and whose food has not changed, have made progress in morality; as for example the Jews, whose sacred books at one time declare that the foul murder of Sisera, by Jael, was an act inspired by God, and later enunciated principles by the mouth of the prophets which show that to them such a deed must have appeared as horrible as it does to us. Evidently, then, the first thing necessary before we can proclaim a morality for humanity is to decide whether there is such a thing as sin for humanity. I do not say sins, but sin; for while the estimate put upon different sins may differ, the important question is, is there such a thing as a sinful condition, of which sins are the particular manifestation.

Let us turn to the Epistle to the Romans. The whole idea is that of election, the calling out of the spiritual man; and the whole conflict of life, we are there told, consists in the effort of the spiritual man to free himself from the "natural" man. Following the Rabbis, Paul declared that the struggling of Jacob and Esau in the womb was a prophecy of the perpetual struggle between the man of flesh and the man of spirit. But he describes the experience of every earnest man when he says, "I know that in me (that is in my flesh) dwelleth no good thing: for to will is present with me, but how to perform that which is present I find not. For the good that I would, I do not, but the evil which I would not, that I do. Now if I do that I would not, it is no more I that do it, but sin that dwelleth in me. I find, then, a law that when I would do good, evil is present with me. For I delight in the law of God after the inward man. But I see another law in my members warring against the law of my mind, and bringing me into captivity to the law of sin which is in my members."

Here, then, is St. Paul's philosophy of sin. God is calling the spiritual man out from the natural man; the conflict of life consists in the holding back of the spiritual man by the flesh, which he calls sin. He afterwards calls this natural man the old Adam. The highest type of the animal life into which God has not breathed the breath of eternal life; and sinfulness, according to Paul, consists in identifying one's self with the old animal life from out of which God is calling man, until the life becomes again "carnal," beastlike. I say we are in a better position to interpret that teaching of St. Paul than ever before. For science has taught us that man has been developed from the lower animal life, and that just in proportion as men have obeyed the better impulse they have left behind the old carnal passions and appetites. Sin, says science, is choosing the lower life from which man has been evolved. If, then, sin be defined as *willful incompleteness*, it is a characteristic of humanity, for there is no man who is not conscious that he is below that which he somehow dimly feels he might have been.

But of course there is no gospel in that. There is need that we should have clearly before us the antipode of sin, and decide whether or not there is a holiness which is for humanity as opposed to the sin of which every individual is now conscious. If we turn to the Epistle to the Ephesians we shall find that St. Paul, who had so emphasized the universality of sin, believed that there was a universal holiness possible for man.

The word that gives the key to that Epistle is "edification" or "upbuilding." Upbuilding to what? "To the measure of the stature of the fullness of Christ." What hinders that? The vanity of mind of those who, having the "understanding darkened, and being alienated from the life of God, have given themselves over to uncleanness." But those who have "learned Christ" will "put off the old man, which is corrupt according to the deceitful lusts, and will put on the new man, which after God is created in righteousness and true holiness." Holiness, then, according to him who has defined sin as *willful incompleteness*, is nothing less than *willing completeness*.

Out of the old beast-like life science and the Bible both tell us man is being called, up to a life which science cannot name, but which the Bible calls the new man, Christ Jesus.

Of course we have reached now a point where argument will have no influence. It is distinctly said that the victory which overcometh the world is faith. But if it be asked why any one should believe that the revelation of Jesus Christ will be to men in every nation the unveiling of an image which has been dimly before their eyes from the beginning, the first reason is that Jesus himself believed it, and it was efficacious; the second is that in proportion as the Church has believed it, has she been able to build men up to this completeness. There is a deeper reason still, of which we shall speak later. If, then, we begin with that faith, we shall see that it is not so unreasonable as we may at first suppose. For the long history of ethics shows us nothing more clearly than this: that men have believed themselves either to be driven on to a better life by some authority which compelled obedience, or that they have been beckoned on by some happiness which seemed to hide itself behind some duty. It must be that there is a truth in each; it must be that neither is complete. What if Christ really combines the two? Yet that is just what the Church has always believed of Him, not because some one has said it, but because individuals are continually experiencing its truth.

The description given of Jesus satisfies these two conditions, "full of grace and truth." To one man it was the grace which appealed; to another, it was the truth that was in Him. It was the "grace" reflected in the face of Philip which drew Nathanael to him, but when he drew near he saw the "truth." The poor wretches who brought the sinful woman into his presence slunk away because of the penalty of his awful majesty. The heart-broken penitent crept to his feet, because she loved the grace of that perfect holiness.

But it was not only the method of Jesus which exhibited these two elements of the power of morality, it was in the end which He set before men as well. He told of a kingdom within each man; He spoke of violated law and unfailing penalty; but He filled the hearts of men with a longing they had never supposed could take possession of them for that peace which is the harmony of righteousness. And then He went a step farther, and showed them one who was at once King and Father, demanding obedience and giving happiness; nay more, identifying obedience and happiness. And the law of that kingdom also was twofold, — love and loyalty.

Of course the objection against this statement is that no external, arbitrary standard can ever suffice for humanity if it is to continue to progress in morality; but the truth is that while Jesus begins with an external standard, it differs from all others in this, that it is the standard of a life, not of a code, and so is not open to the objection urged, because the object of the external standard is to reveal the internal personal standard which is in every man by reason of his sonship. Therefore so far from hindering progress, it insures progress; for morality having once been identified with the love of a son to the Father, the Father having been revealed as eternal, the knowledge of that love must deepen more and more as the exhibition of it becomes more apparent, and the application of it must increase as the knowledge of the relation of one son to another in the great family grows more and more plain in the consciences of men. Therefore while it is true that no morality which in its application is limited can ever satisfy the wants of a progressing humanity, it is equally true that the morality of Jesus can never be insufficient, because it is based on the revelation of the identity of the King and the Father,[1] on the oneness of duty and happiness, on the identity of loyalty and love. This, then, is the

---

[1] See *The Influence of Jesus*, by Phillips Brooks.

standard of "completeness," the perfection like that of the Father in heaven.

This morality, then, beginning with faith proceeds to love and leads on to hope. That last is essential; for the holding up of any standard which either threatens penalty or promises happiness is worse than useless, if it does not reveal a possibility of compliance with its demands. What can be the revelation which can reveal to man the possibility of attaining to the divine perfection? Nothing but that which is the revelation of Jesus, the identity of nature between the Human and the Divine. By this revelation every man may see himself as his Father would have him be. Jesus stands before every life as a mirror stands before a child but half awake, — the child sees an image which it does not recognize, and then, as the light grows clearer, it sees that it is gazing on itself. When man sees Jesus, he sees himself free from sin, fully alive to his relationship to God. So by the power of hope the standard has changed from the outside to the inside. There has come that which St. Paul experienced: "Though I have known Christ after the flesh, yet henceforth I know Him so no more. Christ dwelleth in me; I live, yet not I, but Christ which dwelleth in me."

Surely we have here a morality which is truly humanitarian, — a morality which is based on the oneness of humanity with God and with itself; which reveals the authority which the soul demands; which gives the happiness that the soul craves; which reveals a standard by which men may guide their steps, by faith in the life which has embodied it;

which shows that the law is within, and that the king is within, and that the kingdom is within; and yet opens the vista of an endless progress in the hope of the increase of the kingdom as it is enlarged under the providence of the Father, until the kingdoms of the world are subject to it, and the Son delivers up the kingdom to God who is the Father, that God may be all in all.

But in this progress man does not remain a passive instrument. He can yield — and is daily tempted to yield — his members as instruments of the old carnal life, or he can identify himself with the new Man, who has crucified the affections and lusts by finding his meat and drink in doing the will of his Father.

It may be said, all this is not pure ethics, but ethics mingled with theology. Whether ethics must not always be so mingled is a question which we cannot enter upon here; but this we may be sure of, that no ethics which have been divorced from theology will ever reform the life of the East, for the Orientals are above all things theologians: and that is why Christian morality will have an attraction for them, rather than any system of utilitarianism. It must begin with theology — as Christian ethics begin.

For who is this Son who reveals our sonship to us? Is He too only a product of evolution moving to something not yet seen? The Gospel says not.

First. In the beginning was the Reason, and the Reason was with God, and the Reason was God.

Secondly. All things were made by Him; and without Him was not anything made that was made.

(So too says science, "Nothing was made without law, the expression of Reason.)

Thirdly. He was in the Kosmos, and the Kosmos was made by Him, and the Kosmos knew Him not. (So too says science, Nature knows only *force*.)

Fourthly. He came unto his own (*i. e.*, to men), and his own received Him not. (Alas! how true a statement of history.)

Fifthly. But as many as received Him, to them gave He power to become the Sons of God, even to them that believe on his name; which were born not of blood, nor of the will of the flesh, nor of the will of man, but of God.

Finally. The Reason was made flesh and dwelt among us, and we have seen his glory, the glory as of the only begotten of the Father, full of grace and truth.

Here, then, is the message of Christianity to humanity, — a message as old as the Church itself, but one which we could never fully understand while we thought of sin as a positive entity, but, through the knowledge of the history of evolution, we have come to understand there is the "soul of good in things evil."

With this gospel we can go to the Gentiles and say all these differences of morality show different stages of evolution out of the beast life to the Christ life. Heretofore each nation has been content simply to perpetuate its own standard, but now you can see one who realized every ethnic ideal, and still lifts the standard of moral progress above humanity.

The hospitality and carelessness of the Japanese are perfected in the Friend of man, who took no thought as to what He should eat and drink. The Chinese imitation of the past is idealized in Jesus' *fulfillment* of the past. Hindu patience and Western activity were united in Him who was led as a lamb to the slaughter, and yet said: "I must work while it is day, the night cometh when no man can work."

And it is only when we so consider the question that we come to appreciate the arrogance with which we have thought of all God's other children. We have actually identified the morality of Jesus with the morality of the West! And yet there is a vast deal of Christ's morality — the passive element in it — which the West has never realized at all. We hear a great deal just now about the impracticability of Christ's law of forgiveness and his views of property; but they are not impracticable to the Oriental mind, and it was to the Orient that Jesus belonged. Any one who will read that beautiful book the "Oriental Christ," by Mozumdar, will be convinced that we have lost our hold on a very essential element in Christ's teaching, and that consciousness will help us to carry the Gospel to the heathen, — not the lesson of English prudence and American smartness, but the law of brotherhood in Jesus Christ. The Church must show that the morality of Jesus, like his theology, comes to individuals at the salient point which they have thrown out.

When that is accepted by the East we shall find something more than moral progress as the result.

We shall find a more distinct spiritual vision. For, first, in that seeing of the perfect man there would come, as always has come, an enthusiasm for humanity, for they would fall in love with humanity's image ; and when that took place pantheism would cease, for in the light of that life men would learn that personal consciousness is higher than impersonal unconsciousness, and so, under the "grace" of Jesus Christ, they would realize their relation to a person, even a Father.

And, secondly, that *fear* which in the East has always been associated with a personal god, because personality to them has always had the element of fickleness, would vanish, as under the influence of that life men began to feel that the secret of Jesus' life was unbroken communion with a *father*, as it began to dawn upon them that this father was the Father of all living, and that the assurance of his love was to be found not in efforts to *bribe* Him, but in the identification of the individual life with the Son in whom He is well pleased.

And, thirdly, that awful sense of the necessity of some atonement for the past would be removed, as under the influence of that life men felt that the atonement *had* been made in the revelation of the essential unity of the human and the divine, and borne witness to, even unto death, by the Son of Man, who knew that the transmuting love of the Father was able to make the sins which were as scarlet white as wool.

And, finally, as the story of the impossibility of the perpetual extinguishment of that life by death found its response in their hearts, there would be a new hope. Hopelessness has been the temper of the Oriental. There was nothing to be gained by progress in the manner of life, for life had no future, and no future was desirable for a life so miserable. Our pulses quicken at the thought of an endless life of progress and unwearied activity, for we have become conscious of an inexhaustible energy, which must make itself felt. But no drearier news could be carried to the Chinese, for example, than that life should have no end. If, then, instead of trying to believe that or anything else they could once be brought to feel the influence of Jesus' life, they would find that ideals had come to them which eternity would be none too long to realize, and in the "power of an endless life" they would experience that hope in the unending progress in the knowledge of God which is the gift of the Spirit of Truth.

I have spoken as if the future were certain, but there are dangers. No mysterious ones, but ones that can be prevented. The first is that knowledge may leave faith behind. If that come to pass the sin will lie at the Church's door. We are living today at the beginning of a new age. Life will never be the same again. Religion can never be the same again. In the centuries to come men will look back on this day as we look back to the days of Copernicus. Religious thought set itself against the Copernican theory, and religious thought became contemptible. Religious thought may set itself against the law of evolution, but it will only succeed in becoming again contemptible. We hear a great deal about defending the "outworks" of Christianity; but if the "outworks" are exploded theories of history, nature, and man, the sooner they fall the sooner will that which remaineth the same yesterday, to-day, and forever be revealed.

Another danger, which needs no comment, is that ignorance may utter itself in dogmatism, and so prevent the coöperation of intelligent religious men in all that makes for righteousness.

We have reason to fear lest heathenism, catching the materialistic spirit of so-called Christian lands, may rest satisfied with "progress." No thoughtful man can visit Japan without seeing that they are in danger of adopting every foreign extravagance, instead of developing under the influence of a new spirit their own dignity and beauty.

What Japan needs is the spirit of Christ to call forth her inherent glory, and if she fails to get that she will become the base imitator of all that is crude and uncouth in American and European civilization.

I know there are to be heard voices which say it is all a dream, Christianity has spent its force. But I look backward over history, and the scientist tells me that every upheaval of nature, every modification in plant and animal, prophesied of the coming of man; that without man the whole scheme of evolution would be meaningless. I look over history. I see empires rise and fall. I hear prophets amongst every people declaring that all the travailing and groaning of humanity is not in vain; that humanity shall conceive and bring forth a Son, and that his name shall be called Emmanuel. I see Jesus, the desire of all nations. I see nineteen centuries of Christian history, and I learn that it has been for the manifestation of the life of Christ. I find that this life has not come to men because they have progressed, but I find that when it has come they have progressed. I find that a handful of Jews accepted Him, and as a result there was born the Catholic Church. The middle wall of prejudice between Jew and Gentile was broken down. I find that the Roman accepted Him, and the position of women was changed. In Him was neither male nor female. I find that America accepted Him, and in his presence slavery became intolerable. There could be no difference between bond and free in the brotherhood of mankind.

Look back over these 1,900 years, and you find that everything has changed, even to the very language of the peoples; and yet, through it all, with the wars of nations and the conflict of churches, there has been the unshaken love for and faith in and gratitude to that Life which men have believed called their souls out of darkness into his marvelous light. Under the influence of that Life we find three things: a deeper knowledge of the character of God; a stronger enthusiasm for humanity; and a continual progress in the understanding of nature. Progress in the knowledge of God, — Father, Son, Spirit.

And now look abroad. It has been permitted us to see the rise and progress of one of the most remarkable religious movements in any age. I refer to the Brahmo Somaj, the theistic Church of India. Beginning in an attempt to revive the monotheistic teaching of certain of the Vedic hymns, it has been drawing slowly but surely nearer to the Christian doctrine of the perfect manifestation of God in Jesus Christ. Space will not permit me to quote extracts from the sermons of that remarkable man Keshub Chunder Sen; but no one can read them without feeling the force of St. Paul's words: "I know that he who hath begun a good work in you will perform it till the day of Jesus Christ."

I know that it may be said, "That is but one point of light in the darkness of heathenism, — it is more likely to die out than to spread." But I have no such fear, for I have seen, as it were, the parable of the spread of the gospel glory in the scenery of India itself.

I once stood on the top of the first range of the Himalayas, and saw, across the great valley, the mountains of the second range, with the mighty Kinchenjunga towering above all. The light of the declining moon was only sufficient to show, at the bottom of the valley, the great mist which, like an old serpent, lay coiled about the base of the ancient hills. And as I stood there, cold and trembling, the air was pierced by a bitter cry from a little child in the darkness of the valley; and, while I listened, as if in answer to this human cry, the topmost peak of Kinchenjunga flushed with a faint pink light, —

"the sun has risen," some one cried, and yet the world was dark as ever; but it was true, the mighty mountain had seen, afar off, the breaking of the day, and glowed and trembled in the new-born light. Soon the whole snowy range was ablaze with glory, and the arrows of light fell thick and fast, and the old serpent was slain, and the valley disclosed in all its beauty and peace. So it is true that only here and there a prophetic soul, towering like a mountain above the common level of our dusk, has flushed with glory at the vision of the new day. But we need not fear that the light will turn back: the soul that knows the power of that Sun of Righteousness knows that He will rise with healing in his wings, until the old serpent of despair is slain, and the valleys of humanity glow in the Dayspring from on high which hath visited us.

If, then, I were asked what has Christianity done for the early Aryan religions, I would answer, It has justified every aspiration of their faith, and has opened a vista of unsuspected glory beyond.

If I were asked what is the future of Christianity, I would answer: As humanity increases in wisdom and stature, in favor with God and man, the consciousness of its sonship will grow stronger and deeper; but it will be an incomplete thing while it is only Occidental. We shall never know its true glory ourselves till East and West meet at the cradle of Jesus, and the Wise Men say, *We have seen his star in the East* and are come to worship Him. Only when the East gives Him its gold and frankincense and myrrh, shall we of the West understand what manner of child this is.

Already wise men in the East are beginning to say, "Where is He that is born the King? We have seen his star in the East." What answer has the Church? Will the answer that any section of it may give satisfy "wise men"? Is not the only witness which can convince the world the oneness of his disciples? There are many who believe they see the nearness of a unity as far nobler than the uniformity of mediævalism as is the "federation of the world" to the national subjection to the Papal See. "It is a hope, cherished by many of the most thoughtful and earnest Christians of our time, that God is preparing the introduction, at last, of some new religious era. . . . What, possibly, is He offering, if only we are ready to receive it, but a grand inaugural of the Spirit throughout Christendom,— an open day of life and love and spiritual brotherhood, in which our narrow confines of bigotry and prejudice shall be melted away, and all the members of Christ's body, holding visibly the Head, shall, visibly, own each other; shining in the light, revealing the Spirit, coöperating in the works of Christ, and living for the common object of establishing his kingdom?"[1]

When that comes the Gospel will be preached to the heathen with power, and in proportion as it is preached will that spirit pervade the Church.

[1] *God in Christ*, by Horace Bushnell, pp. 279 and 297.

To have all men see the *fellowship* of the mystery which from the beginning hath been hid in Him who created all things by Jesus Christ may seem to some a dream, but to those who know Him it is the

<blockquote>
One far off divine event
To which the whole creation moves.
</blockquote>

www.ingramcontent.com/pod-product-compliance
Lightning Source LLC
Chambersburg PA
CBHW032055220426
43664CB00008B/1005